small group leadership

AS SPIRITUAL DIRECTION

Practical Ways to Blend an Ancient Art into Your Contemporary Community

HEATHER WEBB

▶ foreword by EUGENE H. PETERSON

ZONDERVAN™

GRAND RAPIDS, MICHIGAN 49530 USA

small group leadership

AS SPIRITUAL DIRECTION

Practical Ways to Blend an Ancient Art Into Your Contemporary Community

HEATHER WEBB

▶ foreword by EUGENE H. PETERSON

Small Group Leadership as Spiritual Direction: Practical Ways to Blend an Ancient Art into Your Contemporary Community
Copyright © 2005 by Youth Specialties

Youth Specialties Books, 300 South Pierce Street, El Cajon, CA 92020, are published by Zondervan, 5300 Patterson Avenue SE, Grand Rapids, MI 49530

Library of Congress Cataloging-in-Publication Data
Webb, Heather.
  Small group leadership as spiritual direction : practical ways to blend an
ancient art into your contemporary community / by Heather P. Webb.
     p. cm.
  Includes bibliographical references (p. 131-144).
  ISBN 0-310-25952-5 (pbk.)
  1. Spiritual direction. 2. Church group work. 3. Christian leadership.
4. Small groups--Religious aspects--Christianity. I. Title.
  BV5053.W42 2005
  253'.7--dc22

                                                                            2004023958

Editorial by Carla Barnhill
Art direction by Jay Howver and Holly Sharp
Editing by Janie Wilkerson
Proofreading by Maureen McNabb and Joanne Heim
Cover design by Rule29
Interior design by SharpSeven
Cover & Interior font: House Gothic™ Copyright © House Industries

Printed in the United States of America

05 06 07 08 09 10 / DC / 10 9 8 7 6 5 4 3 2 1

For Alyse,
my beloved daughter,
who every day teaches me more of God's heart

For my parents and my husband's parents
who have been wise spiritual directors to us in our journey:
Betsy, Geoff, Betty, and Kenneth

TABLE OF CONTENTS

SECTION 1: Small Groups: Coming Together for Relationship

SECTION 2: Spiritual Direction: Reviving the Ancient Art

SECTION 3: Direction as a Small Group Leadership Style

SECTION 4: New Models for a New Era

Spiritual direction is language used in the context of the twin mysteries of the soul and God. Prayer, language used in conversation between the soul and God, is our primary language. Spiritual direction, language used between and among "souls" in the company of God, is a sister language. It is language used in reverence, conveying wonder (there is so much beyond us!) and embracing ambiguity (there is so much we don't know!). The language of prayer and spiritual direction have this in common: language (whether in words or silence) in the Presence, in the context of mystery, listening for and hinting at "what eye has not seen nor ear heard" (1 Corinthians 2:9) and "the love of Christ that surpasses knowledge" (Ephesians 3:19).

+

Emily Dickinson once said that mystery is the greatest need in the human soul. So what happens to us—especially those of us whose lives are shaped by belief in God, "immortal, invisible, God only wise / in light inaccessible hid from our eyes"—when the vocabulary and syntax of mystery have been excised from our language and the only words left to us for conversing about God and our souls have to do with function and information? We ask God to do something (reducing God to a function) or ask him what he is doing (giving him a job as clerk in an information booth). But not with the happiest of results. Anyone who ventures to ask God for anything at all is soon asking parents or pastors or friends why there is "no answer." But there is an answer. Spiritual direction is in the business of discerning the signs of God's work and attending to the way that God answers.

+

William Stafford is an American poet who has explored the intuitive dimensions of language as well as anyone I know. He writes of people who "want a wilderness with a map." Most of us have become accustomed to a life that is laid out on streets, each designated by a number or a name, each building and residence given an address to which mail can be delivered. We like the ordered predictability of village and city life. We want to know where things are and how we can get to them. But we also, from time to time, get a little bored by it—we miss the element of surprise and discovery that gave so much zest to our fondly remembered childhood. And so we go looking for adventure. We play or watch a game, read a novel, go to a movie, travel to Zanzibar. One of the classic ways of restoring a sense of wonder tinged with adventure, the sheer mystery of life, is to enter the wilderness—a world blessedly free of domestication, permeated by what we don't know: mountains that defy our control, weather indifferent to our comfort, grizzly bears and mountain lions unpredictable and dangerous. Life spills out of the containers of our routines. In the wilderness we become alert; we can take nothing for granted: every tree is a live sculpture, every flower a surprise, every animal a grace, each step taking us into a never-before-experienced combination of scent and color and shape. Our simple sense of life, basic life, is heightened. Boredom is banished.

+

Except. Except that many of us soon find the mystery—the lack of control, the lack of comfort, the lack of security—unsettling. We would like the fresh new lease on the glories of being alive in God's world but without mystery. We are the ones who William Stafford castigates in his fine phrase as those who "want a wilderness with a map": we want to know where we are, we want to know what to expect, we want to be in control. But if we know where we are and what to expect and are in control, we are not in the wilderness. We may as well be back in town with stop lights and signs telling us when to stop and go, with house numbers defining our location, and with a doctor conveniently on call if we happen to break a leg.

+

Stafford's "wilderness with a map" describes a great deal of what goes on in the Christian church these days. We think we want God beyond our understanding so we can worship largely, God sovereign in all our circumstances and suffering so we can be cared for securely, the God of Paul's exclamatory, "How unsearchable are his judgments and how inscrutable his ways!" (Romans 11:33). But then we get nervous about the "unsearchable" and the "inscrutable." We hesitate, maybe that's just a little too much mystery. We hesitate, get cold feet, pull back. We want a "wilderness with a map."

And so we send in bulldozers to clear roads through the mystery, straight and narrow doctrines, so we know where we are. Then we erect signs that tell us what we need to look for and what to be wary of. Soon there is no wilderness, no mystery. We know all that we need to know—what we believe is all defined for us. We know exactly what to do and when to do it—proper behavior is clearly sign-posted. But there is a problem. After the bulldozers have done their work and the engineers have erected their signs there is no mystery. We are in control.

Spiritual direction, directing or being directed in matters of God and the soul, is the practice of using language regarding things we don't know very much about, language that does not strive for mastery, language that slowly but surely becomes comfortable with mystery. We come to Jesus wanting answers and miracles, and he most certainly gives answers and does miracles—but rarely on the terms in which we expect them. Answers for us consist of information we can use; miracles are shortcuts around difficulties that have us stumped. Information is the secularized substitute for God's answers and technology is the secularized substitute for God's miracles. Spiritual direction is the cultivation of language that pays attention to the way God answers, and the way God performs miracles.

Is it any wonder that we need help in acquiring a language appropriate to mystery? All our lives we have gone to schools that have equated mystery with ignorance, schools promising to banish ignorance from our lives if we will just study hard enough. If there is a sense within us that there is something other than that which we need for our salvation, we are given another book to read or invited to sign up for another academic degree.

There are many advantages that accrue when we use language to "say" things clearly: announce truth, give commands, define the world around us, explain how men and women think or feel, plan a day's work, apply for a job, write a computer manual, make a will, prepare a contract, give directions to a distant city, and also (most importantly) formulate Christian doctrine and guide moral behavior. But if that is the only way we know how to use language, we leave out too much, far too much. For there is much about life that is not "sayable" in the ways in which we use language to navigate through our workplaces, our schools, our shopping malls, and our churches. There are huge mysteries in which we are immersed from the moment we come out of the womb. There are complex ambiguities that cannot be sorted out by definitions, explanation, directions, and exhortations.

Spiritual direction is another way of language, a way of approaching the mystery of our lives. It is the practice of providing a safe time and place in which the mysteries of God and the soul are honored—not reduced to problems, not explained as symptoms. It is a way of language rooted in the biblical revelation and in continuous use in our 2,000 years of living in Christian community. The soul by its very nature resists being understood as a category or class: just beneath the surface we are all bundles of uncharted idiosyncrasies. And God by his very nature cannot be contained in a definition: one of our ancestors said it well, "A God who can be understood is not God."

+

This is the work to which Dr. Heather Webb has given years of passionate attention. It is what she goes to work each day to practice in the small groups in which she gathers and the classrooms in which she teaches. Immersed as we are in a culture that understands personal relationships almost exclusively in psychological terms, it is very difficult to establish a quite different (biblical) perspective and to bring it off with coherence and accuracy. But she does it. Reading this book will acquaint you with what she does and how she does it, this practice that is so essential to the health of the Christian community today. Hopefully, you will join her along with an increasing number of men and women in the neighborhoods and congregations of our land who are quietly meeting with others to practice listening to the ways in which God speaks to us, practicing the language of the soul as we respond to God, language quite different from what we use in our shopping and workplace, language which more often that not is expressed in "sighs too deep for words" (Romans 8:26).

Eugene H. Peterson
Professor Emeritus of Spiritual Theology
Regent College, Vancouver B.C. Canada

INTRODUCTION

"What is my calling?"

"Should I marry the person I'm dating?"

"What am I doing with my life?"

"Why do I feel so alone?"

"Why doesn't anyone understand me?"

"Do I matter in the world?"

"Who is God in my life?"

Questions like these are the cries of all who long for their lives to connect with a broader story, with God. These questions are profoundly personal, yet inherently relational. They are the kinds of questions people ask of their most trusted friends, those whom they believe will listen thoughtfully and advise carefully. They are reflections of an ache for meaning and a craving for a life that matters. They proceed from the hunger of souls seeking the sacred.

In today's church environment, this soul hunger is often met by the concept of the small group. And so it is often in the context of the small group that questions like those listed above are raised. While some groups are able to process these questions quite naturally, I find that many small group leaders feel bewildered by these raw, intimate concerns. They ask themselves, *Am I supposed to provide an answer? How can I speak for God in this person's life? What are they asking of the group? Of me? How do we respond?*

It is precisely in this place of terror that the companionship of community finds its power. The small group setting invites people to share their stories of faith, to journey with others who are on the same path. Small groups answer both the need for relationships (opportunities to know and be known) and presence (our own, others', and God's). In the most effective small groups, the participants are able to join one another in the quest to find answers to their deepest questions. But doing so will require a new paradigm in our vision of group leadership.

Spiritual direction is the ancient art of being with another person in their relationship with God. As the church struggles to be a place in which we develop meaningful and lasting relationships, this spiritual practice has much to offer. It is another way of patiently sitting with another soul as we listen for God's voice and look for God's leading. Answers to life's difficult questions can come in the space direction creates between people who are present to one another in the presence of God.

SECTION 1

SMALL GROUPS: COMING TOGETHER FOR RELATIONSHIP

SOUL HUNGER

From the bestseller list to the growing number of stores featuring self-help books on meditation, yoga, and centering, it's obvious that the last few years have brought a dramatic increase in spiritual curiosity and hunger. Even those who are loath to assign themselves a religious label are exploring the spiritual realm with increasing passion. And yet there is a sense in which the Christian church is failing to meet this hunger with a real, meaningful response.

Consider the movie *Dogma*. Ben Affleck and Matt Damon play fallen angels who are trying to find their way back to heaven by way of a moral loophole. In one scene, Affleck's character talks to a young woman, Bethany, who is on a pilgrimage she doesn't understand. She doesn't realize she's speaking with a fallen angel. She's been drinking, which prompts her to speak more plainly than she might normally have done. Listen to what she says:

Angel: *You still go to church?*
Bethany: *Every Sunday.*
Angel: *Does it do anything for you?*
Bethany: *It gives me time to balance my checkbook every week.*
Angel: *See, that's what I'm saying. I mean, people don't go to church to feel spiritual anymore. They go to church and feel bored. But they keep going every week just out of habit. When do you think you lost your faith?*

> Bethany: I remember the exact moment. I was on the phone with my mother. And she was trying to counsel me through this thing. And nothing she was saying was making me feel any better. She said, "Bethany, God has a plan." I was so angry with her. I was like, What about my plans? You know?
>
> Angel: Uh-huh.
>
> Bethany: I had planned to have a family with my husband. Wasn't that plan good enough for God? Apparently not. What about you? When did you lose your faith?
>
> Angel: A long time ago. One day God just stopped listening. I kept talking, but I got the distinct impression that he wasn't listening anymore.
>
> Bethany: How did you know she was listening in the first place?
>
> Angel: I guess I don't.
>
> Bethany: I hate thoughts like that. You know, they come to you with age because when you're a kid, you never question the whole faith thing. Um-um. God's in heaven and he's—she's always got her eye on you. I'd give anything to feel that way again. Guess that's why I got talked into this pilgrimage.[1]

These characters ask the crucial question, "Does the church do anything for us?" There is a sense that both Bethany and the Angel wish the answer were yes. This conversation reflects the longing found in the hearts of the faithful and the faithless alike. Faith is lost not because there is no need for it, but because we believe God's plans don't make any sense. In fact, Bethany notes that not only do they not make sense, but they seem cruel and arbitrary as well.

In essence, these characters are saying the church doesn't meet us. It doesn't meet our needs, our desires, our hopes, or our hunger. The church doesn't connect with us. And when we sense that the church doesn't connect, we move on to the belief that God can't connect with us either.

When I first saw this scene, I was convicted. I have likely said to someone in pain, "God's going to take care of it," or "God meant it for good." But notice how Bethany connects that sentiment with the moment she lost her faith. Yet she hasn't lost the desire for faith; this scene bears evidence that a hunger for God exists even when belief seems to fall away. We glimpse Bethany's heart as she says, "I'd give anything to feel that way again." That's soul hunger.

I don't believe the church has intentionally ignored this soul hunger. The church has used education to teach us about matters of faith. It has created communities in which we can learn the ways of faith. It is a source of fellowship so we can journey with others on a path of faith. But there must be something more we can offer to invite these spiritual seekers to Christian community. What would be required to meet that woman on the train, to meet her heartache?

There are large segments of the population that are dissatisfied with the church, wounded by the institution. They are trying to find room in their theology for the questions and doubt that have surfaced in the course of their lives. It is a critical time for the church to honor the seekers, to invite them to God and community in the midst of their wanderings, not once they get it all figured out. The spiritual hunger of this age presents an opportunity for us to offer a seat at the table and a cup of warm soup to those who know they are in need.

Contours of soul hunger

Of course, addressing this spiritual hunger means understanding the ways in which this hunger is lived out in the lives of seekers. There are several common markers that we as the church need to recognize as we look for ways to invite people like Bethany into the church.

The first marker is what British theologian Dave Tomlinson calls a "pick and mix"[2] belief system. It can resemble a fast-food convenience store— get a little of this and a little of that. That's why many seekers are comfortable mixing principles from Judaism, Buddhism, and Hinduism into the basic expressions of Christianity. It is just as easy to read the latest news on the Dalai Lama as it is to find out what the Bible says on an afterlife. This challenges us to redefine what is essential to being a Christian rather than assuming the only legitimate expression of faith is one that adheres to all elements of the Christian subculture.

A positive effect of this pick-and-mix mentality is that seekers are relatively comfortable with ambiguity. Mark Yaconelli, a spiritual director, notes that with Generation X-ers, "there's a whole aspect to their spiritual life that the Christian faith will have to be experiential, anti-institutional, address suffering, and be ambiguous which is the word for mystery."[3] Gen X-ers can hold two opposite concepts of something with equal validity, not either/or but both/and. Reality needn't be defined in black and white.

In many ways, this frees the church to embrace the mystery of God, to allow for God to be expansive and awesome rather than some definable entity. No longer is there a need to "prove" the un-provable that is faith. Now there is more room for the experiential and supernatural. There is room for God to work in ways that are outside of our understanding. Faith can therefore draw people not by propositional argument but by lived invitations to share stories and appreciate each other as fellow travelers on the faith journey, not objects of another's coercion.

A second marker is the importance of relationship. We are in a state of near-constant change. New technology, transportation, information, and mobility ensure that today will be different from yesterday. Ironically, even as the world gets "smaller" because of technology, the pace at which we travel and function brings with it a profound sense of isolation for Postmoderns. There is a felt estrangement from others, particularly as we become more hidden behind our Wi-Fi networks and iPods.

This sense of isolation brings with it a kind of spiritual unrest. Despite our unprecedented consumption of goods and resources, rest and contentment remain elusive. Most spiritual seekers have experienced dissatisfaction, even disillusionment, with our consumerist culture. With so many options they find that even choice itself becomes meaningless.

Henri Nouwen spoke to where we find ourselves: "Traditional ways of living are breaking down. And we are more than ever thrown back on our own personal resources."[4] Yet, we know we can't survive on our own. So we seek out community, relationships with others who we believe will somehow join their stories with ours so that together we can create something meaningful.

What an opportunity for the church! We are at a point in history when the longing for faith, for meaning, is on the rise. We are faced with a population hungry for connection, for relationship, for a sense of belonging to something bigger than themselves. If we are willing to rethink our assumptions about faith and the church, we can offer the hungry masses a faith feast of unimaginable proportions.

Obviously, there are numerous ways for the church to tap into the need and desires of this seeking populace. Some will demand we make radical changes; others may call for only minor tweaking. I believe one of the most effective tools the church has in hand is the small group.

CHAPTER TWO

CHRISTIAN COMMUNITY

Over the years, students in my counseling classes have told me that the relational experiences they have in their small groups are just what they longed for in their church communities but weren't sure how to achieve.[5] There is something unique about a small group. At its best, it is made up of people gathering with a common goal: to be trained to love better and relate to others in more powerful ways.

These people come with a desire to learn about themselves and are open to feedback in the group setting. They are willing to risk receiving from and offering to one another despite their uncertainty about how they will be perceived. Tears and laughter are shared and celebrated. There is a delightful sense of freedom about these kinds of groups as people begin to live into their dreams. In some ways, small groups are Outward Bound for the soul. They engage all of our senses and demand that we stay present and open to others.

At the same time, groups can disintegrate into places of harm or neglect. When a group becomes stagnant, closes itself off to the outsider, or defines itself by narrow ideologies, the small group can be reduced to an exclusive social club. It takes a clear vision and sense of purpose for a small group to remain true to its focus of nurturing souls and deepening relationships. It takes a strong spiritual leader to guide the group toward Christian community, even when it is difficult.

In my experience, people are innately drawn to small groups. From childhood, we seek out those who are like us, those with whom we share a common interest. As we get older, we become more open to the idea that we can create groups based on shared values or lifestyles—professional fellowship groups, quilting classes, or service organizations. Even the disenfranchised pull together in small groups—think of the punk movement or goth culture. They may share little but their disaffection with the culture, yet they find in one another a sense of belonging and community.

Because we naturally gravitate toward small groups, it makes sense that the church has adopted them as a means of spiritual formation. And while this discussion will focus primarily on small groups within the Christian community, it's important to note that small groups often develop in non-formal settings as well. One of my formative small group experiences took place right after college. I moved several states away from my college friends and was eager to find fellowship in my new home. Through word of mouth, I found out about a group of 20-somethings who met for a Bible study. We were an eclectic bunch. Some of us went to church, some didn't. None of us was in full-time ministry, but most of us volunteered with local Young Life or youth groups. We had no formal training in theology or biblical exegesis; we were just curious, hungry people believing God might be up to something in our lives.

For church-based groups, there is the connection to the larger mission of the church. The broader church can provide theological grounding, support for the leaders, a network of resources, and a place to fulfill other aspects of a Christian's life in community. Groups outside the church can awaken a desire in members to be connected to history, liturgy, and tradition through a larger body.

While we tend to think of small group ministry as a relatively new concept in the church, the practice actually dates back to the beginning of the Christian faith. In the early church, Christians invited people to a faith marked by how they lived and how they loved one another. In Acts 4, we are told that the first Christians had a communal view of care for each other and those marginalized by society. "All the believers were one in heart and mind. No one claimed that any of his possessions was his own, but they shared everything they had...and it was distributed to anyone as he had need" (vs. 32, 35).They were missionaries, tentmakers, merchants, landowners, and crusaders for truth. They shared a common heart for following in the way of Jesus and for preaching God's redeeming love for all people. They were diverse people from different cultures, classes, and races, but with a shared vision of faith and community.

The New Testament understanding of the church as the body of Christ—a metaphor of connection—offers another view of the value of the small group. In 1 Corinthians 12, we hear more about this body that God has lovingly fashioned together as a unified whole. Even in the midst of diversity, our goal is that "there should be no division in the body, but that its parts should have equal concern for each other. If one part suffers, every part suffers with it; if one part is honored, every part rejoices with it" (vs. 25-26). There is a built-in need within the church for us to share our burdens and celebrate our triumphs with one another.

Jesus provides a powerful picture of life in community. He took on human flesh, dwelt among us, and chose 12 somewhat unsavory characters to be his most intimate community. He called them his family. This band of followers traveled, ate, slept, listened, and prayed with Jesus. They witnessed their leader being betrayed, beaten, condemned, exposed, and crucified. They were meant to journey with him in the times of jubilation and defeat.

When we look back on the early church or on Jesus' community of disciples, it's tempting to see only the good that comes from life lived in connection with others. And yet the letters of the Apostle Paul point to the near-constant tension of the early Christian communities. We are self-centered people for whom living in community does not come naturally. We want our own way, we want to be in charge, we want to live our own lives without having to answer to others. Imagine life as a disciple: leaving behind your livelihood to follow someone who incites crowds and claims to be the Son of God. Imagine life in the early church: offering all you've earned to the communal pot, living by a code of behavior that defies everything you've been taught. Community life demands that we live in ways that go against our human nature.

Still, the disciples, the early church, and those of us who seek out the small group experience all believe we are meant for community. We trust that life in the body of Christ is the best way for us to become the people God created us to be. We believe we will be transformed in the process of sharing our lives with others. Being open to God's intrusions in our lives through relationships with others is a radical first step toward embracing the call to be a changed people.

CHAPTER THREE

TODAY'S SMALL GROUPS

Today's small groups fit both traditional and non-traditional models. Church and parachurch groups represent a more traditional approach. They are extensions of the church community, places in which the call to fellowship is lived out through intimate relationships. Many churches place great importance on having all their members join a small group. In megachurches, small groups often play a vital role in helping people feel connected to the larger body. Because they are made up of people who already have something in common—attendance at the same church, similar life stage, interest in a particular topic—these traditional groups are often quite homogeneous.

That's not necessarily the case with non-traditional groups, which have come on the scene more recently and are growing in popularity around the country. These groups often look like the one I was involved in after college. They are made up of friends, or coworkers, or friends of friends who come together with some kind of common interest in spiritual issues. They may do a Bible study, read spiritual classics, or work through other spiritual practices such as centering prayer or even yoga.

The *Wall Street Journal* took note of this trend, saying, "In a move to deepen their spiritual lives, some Americans are tackling a new do-it-yourself project: religion... .Today's do-it-yourselfers are modern versions of the Christian 'house churches' and Jewish havurah (friendship) groups that emerged in the 60's."[6] There are, however, potential drawbacks to this model. As non-traditional groups grow in popularity, they can encounter the same problems as more traditional groups: space, marketing, fundraising...[7] They can also be a limited substitute for more substantial church affiliation, which means group members may miss out on other important aspects of the Christian experience (the sacraments, service and mission, theological education, etc.).

Still, the church needs to understand the role of these small groups, inside and outside their walls, and appreciate the spiritual hunger of those who attend. I once attended a group in which the members felt disenfranchised from a local conservative congregation. They valued many of their relationships from the church but felt they had to go outside to find spiritual sustenance. A prison chaplain agreed to come in from another town and meet with this group every month and have a fellowship/worship time with them. It was set up as a transitional community that had the possibility of sending members back into a local church. It has continued for eight years even as some members have gotten plugged in to other churches. It has proven to be a place where those with a deep desire for Christian community can find it even while they search for a connection with a church to call home.

People find these small groups through the Internet, word of mouth, and invitations at seminaries or academic institutions. The meeting places are typically open to others, newcomer-friendly, and easy to find. The 20-something group I attended after college came together because the two organizers, a pair of brothers, asked their friends who were thinking about faith and had questions to come together to look at the Bible twice a month. It was outreach in the best sense of the word. They included friends from high school, college, their workplaces, area teachers, other corporate types they met on the commuter train, and a few musicians connected to an underground network of music people asking spiritual questions. That group had a seeker-sensitive focus but took issues of faith seriously.

There are as many examples of diverse, out-of-the-box groups as there are groups gathered. There are many that view themselves as missional, designed to be seeker-sensitive as well as functioning as a small group that cares for one another's needs. I know of several book clubs that read various kinds of literature but do so in the context of considering questions of life and faith together with friends and neighbors who may or may not come from a faith perspective. Dave Tomlinson writes of an experience in his life that rekindled his passion for the church (in all her forms). He met at a local pub with a group of people who felt themselves to be outside the church for a variety of reasons. Over a pint, they were free to share life, stories, doubts, questions, and frustrations. There were no thought-police at the pub.[8] The freedom they found allowed many to return to more traditional forms of church with a newfound sense of desire because of what they shared in those informal gatherings.

Given today's spiritual climate, out of which future small group members will arise, it is obvious a leader or facilitator needs new gifts beyond just being a good teacher and discussion leader. Groups are gathering not only for those with a commitment to a church body but also as an entry point for seekers to start connecting with churches (or even form something new entirely). Today's small group leaders have the opportunity to act as spiritual directors for their groups.

CHAPTER FOUR

SMALL GROUPS AND SPIRITUAL NEEDS

The power of small groups is found in the dynamic of those gathered together around a common desire: to know God and others more deeply and to be known in those relationships as well. However, there are limits to what small groups can accomplish. It's essential for us to understand the parameters of the small group before we develop a model of leadership.

The place of Scripture

To begin with, we need to allow the small group to be *a* means of spiritual formation, but never expect it to be the *only* means. I remember a gathering of our small group where someone asked, "If we really believe this stuff, then aren't we supposed to sell all we have, wander down the road, confident that God will send someone to pick us up and feed us?" That question was asked by one of the artists in the group and caused visible discomfort for the "yuppies" present. We thought we were supposed to get jobs, start pension funds, be responsible, and settle down. We were startled into silence. Without any real sense of how to read or understand the Bible, we were left to our own devices and all the limitations that implies.

In many ways, it was better for us to acknowledge our ignorance and wade through our admittedly limited understanding of the Bible together rather than claim expertise and lead ourselves down a path of faulty theology.

When a small group sees itself as the dispenser of biblical or doctrinal truths, it is venturing into waters that dilute the power of the group.

Small groups are not teaching environments. Rather, they represent a group of people encountering one another and listening for God's guiding Spirit. That is not to say people are not learning theology along the way. However, small groups are most successful when they are about people on a mutual journey of discovering God's work in their lives.

Apart from the obvious concerns about small groups taking on the role of theologians, there are also practical issues. When a small group takes on the mantle of theological training, it assumes a more hierarchical structure. Someone is knowledgeable and the others become students, no longer able to teach but only to absorb the wisdom dispensed from another. It is the "expert" model of training rather than one of equipping the body to be "the royal priesthood" of believers (1 Peter 2:9).

At the same time, the Bible is an essential member of any group that is centered on life with God. It is helpful, then, for groups to determine how they want to incorporate the biblical text into their group times. In other words, groups need to develop a hermeneutical approach that offers them a way of reading and using God's Word that is faithful to the author (both the divine and human authors), the text (its historical and cultural implications), and the reader (our experiences, biases, and worldviews).

The place of the reader is particularly important in considering the purpose of small groups. The focus on the reader asks, "Who am I when I approach the text? How will I let it impact my life? What questions do I bring today? What openness or prejudice do I bring to the task of reading?" We all have biases, ideas, and opinions that color our reading of the text. We have to consider whether it is possible to completely remove our presuppositions and read the Bible objectively. In other words, did Jesus ask people to come to him with their stories, sufferings, and celebrations or to "get over it" and be objective as they grew toward a relationship with him?

Of course the danger of reading Scripture through the lens of our experiences and worldviews is that we can often miss what God has to say to us. Our prejudices can get in the way of God's Word calling us to new lives—we want to see ourselves as the Good Samaritan, not the priest who passes by. That's why reading in community can have such a powerful influence. When we include the voices of others, we begin to get a fuller picture of what God has to say through the Bible and how we might go about finding ourselves in God's story of redemption.

My husband and I were in a couples' Bible study where we decided to tackle Ecclesiastes. As we began the process of reading the first chapter, many of the men began groaning aloud with the words, "All is vanity." I found I was having a different experience with this passage; I had a sense of all things flowing back to God. I was actually comforted by the words. I was also recovering from a significant time of grief in my life, so these words spoke to me in a new, life-giving way.

However, I found myself not wanting to share my reaction, because it was not what the others were feeling. Toward the end of our time, I finally expressed my response to the passage. Although some in the group looked at me as if I had a very different version of the same text, one other voice spoke to the fact that he, too, found something mysterious, yet compelling, about this chapter that helped him gain a new perspective on life. The fact that we had a variety of perspectives allowed us all to grasp a richer meaning in the text. I learned more of the male sense of futility as well as the mystery of the text, and the others were able to entertain other angles on Ecclesiastes as well.

Integrity in reading requires that we have respect for the intent of the author and divine author as well as the words of the text and our own hearts as readers. What is it I uniquely bring that might matter as we gather to read God's Word? Perhaps if I do not speak, others will miss something the Spirit desires to bring to us in the process.

We will spend more time on the definition of spiritual direction in future chapters; however, it is helpful to note that effective direction includes understanding the importance of the individual's experience with God's Word. The gathering of God's people, even those seeking and uncertain of their faith, is an opportunity for people to come, taste, and see that the Lord is good. This is done not only by direct contact with the Scriptures (if they are used in a specific group), but also by the indirect encounter with the Word as it is lived out in the lives of those present.

The place of honesty

There is much to be gained when the family of God gathers together in an effort to seek God and know God's ways. And yet, small groups often fail when they focus too heavily on gaining knowledge and understanding and sacrifice the equally important need for spiritual refreshment. Jesus used the law to convict sinners of sin in his perfect, sinless way, but he also used it to invite people to receive God's soul care. Jesus was concerned that the religious wise men of his day understood much of the letter of the law but lacked a heart for the spirit of what God intended.

Paul's words in 2 Corinthians 3:6 speak to this truth: "He has made us competent as ministers of a new covenant—not of the letter but of the Spirit; for the letter kills, but the Spirit gives life." This truth invites us to think of God's Spirit and presence as life-giving and to engage in honest, care-filled community. Brian McLaren describes it this way: "Conversation implies a real relationship, and if we make our goal to establish relationships and engage in authentic conversations, I know that conversions will happen. But if we keep trying to convert people, we'll simply drive them away. They are sick of our sales pitches and our formulas."[9]

There is power in creating authentic community with one another. Ideally a small group becomes a place where its members can drop the masks of performance and perfection so often demanded by our culture. Instead, they can be themselves. This chance to be fully known by others can be one of the most spiritually nurturing experiences of community life.

Creating that kind of refreshment necessitates an atmosphere of trust and mutual respect. In the chapters to come we will look at the challenges of being people who speak the truth in love, who are open to the outsider, who invite others to join in the life Jesus offers when he says, "Whoever believes in me, as the Scripture has said, streams of living water will flow from within him." (John 7:38). We must allow ourselves to be people who come wanting, needing, and asking that Jesus find us and fill us.

CHAPTER FIVE

SMALL GROUP DYNAMICS

Since every group is made up of individuals with their own stories, groups are inherently complex organisms. People bring their issues from the past, hopes for the future, and confusion about the present. They bring their insecurities and their desires to be seen, known, and loved. They want to be included, yet they want to stand out. They act in profoundly caring ways, yet also act in irrational and alienating ways. The job of a spiritual director is to sort all this out, or at least invite the group into the process of sorting it out, and to try to weave a tapestry of connection in which the group can participate and celebrate.

This involves a solid understanding of the subtleties of group dynamics. When we were kids, my siblings and I often battled over the prime seat in the car, trying to be the first to "call it." For some reason, we never "called it" the night before or even an hour before we were supposed to leave the house. There was some kind of ingrained understanding that the bidding didn't begin until we were out the door and on our way to the car. Often a parent was brought in to mediate competing claims, but the rights issue was clear. There was a pecking order that needed to be maintained.

Most adults have stopped claiming "shotgun," but we all know that whenever people gather, there are more interpersonal dynamics at play than are obvious on the surface. In fact, there are many elements, seen and unseen, that set into motion the ways in which members of a small group will interact with one another.

Over the years I've found it interesting to watch how a group of students react when they come into a roomful of chairs that all look alike with the exception of one or two more comfortable chairs. For the first week the nicer seats are usually left for the group leader or facilitator. After a week or two the deferential practice is abandoned and people start to claim the nicer chairs, often with the help of an offhand comment like, "My back is sore today," or "I have to share today so I thought I should be comfortable," or "This is closest to the door and I need to leave early." We somehow do not feel we merit the better seats and therefore need to have reasons to have chosen them over others. Still, I am always amazed at how quickly something as mundane as a comfortable chair can change the dynamics of a group. Those who sit in the comfortable chairs tend to talk more and often become more outspoken in their opinions than they were when they sat in the regular chairs.

My classroom experiment is a simple example of the complicated stages most small groups work through during their tenure. There is a beginning point, a middle, and an end that most groups journey through, whether they meet for eight weeks or eight years. There is no standard for how long the stages last, but what is clear is that each one shifts the dynamics of the group, sometimes a little, sometimes a lot. Regardless, leaders need to be prepared to guide the group through these times of change.

Getting to know you: The vision stage

In the first few meetings, groups create patterns. This means most people find their relational place and will occupy it for the remainder of their time with the group. They discover the group's talkers and its listeners. People find themselves drawn to some members and cautious or withdrawn around others. They develop a sense of who is likely to see their perspective and who isn't. They decide how they'll live in this group and outside of it. Obviously, much of this takes place on a subconscious level, but as everyone settles in and an atmosphere of trust is created, these feelings may surface in the form of thoughtful questioning or self-reflection.

It is in this early stage of group life that some important issues need to be decided and agreed upon. One of the first decisions of a group is to determine why they are meeting— their mission and purpose. Even within the structure of a church, small groups meet for different reasons. Some study a book together, some meet to pray, some gather solely to encourage one another's faith and develop friendships. Whatever the group's purpose, it's important for it to be communicated clearly from the beginning.

My friend David left the third meeting of his men's group feeling discouraged. He wondered why he sensed a tug-of-war between different members of the group. He had started the group with the idea that it would be a place for young fathers to pray for each other and support one another. Now it seemed like each person wanted something different. Ted kept trying to get them to read a book that had impacted him. Ryan wanted them to discuss some of the leadership dynamics at church and brainstorm ways of dealing with them. John was one of the church's associate ministers. He didn't say much during the meetings but seemed both irritated and sad. David felt like a failure. He had thought by inviting this group of guys to come together they would find their way and eventually get on the same page. Instead, they were splitting apart and irritated at him for not taking charge.

David's situation is not uncommon. He had an idea of what he hoped for, but the group itself never bought into his vision. David had not wanted to lead or assert control in the beginning, so each member created his own agenda, and the group fell apart.

The process of determining a group's vision often happens before the group even forms. Someone gets an idea or feels led to start a group and invites others to join in with that idea. But even in those groups in which someone "owns" the vision, it's important for the whole group to contribute to the trajectory of living out that vision.

Vision casting is a process of give and take. It requires the willingness to sacrifice part of my plan and agenda for the good of yours. When the group process is allowed to take over, the end result is often finer than what was originally envisioned by each of the individuals. Having watched many groups work together, I have seen that a collective has a power beyond what one person alone can offer. It is something wonderful and fascinating to behold.

On a practical level, the group needs to determine its primary task, be it working through a book, encouraging one another's faith, dealing with addiction, developing friendships, prayer, or Bible study. They need to talk about whether they want to be an open or closed group. Closed means the group is committed to one another for a certain length of time and can choose to change or add new members after that point. The group also needs to work out logistics: how often they'll meet and where, how they will structure their time together, that kind of thing.

The group will also need to make decisions about leadership. They may want to choose one person as a group facilitator or have a regular discussion leader. They may want to take turns leading the discussion or planning the time. It is also important for groups to talk early on about how they want to handle conflict within the group. Setting out expectations before problems arise helps everyone know what to expect and can help members resolve issues before they damage the group.

This is all part of casting a vision for the group. Often, as groups talk about who they want to be, they also talk about who they *don't* want to be. In the process, the group moves toward creating a corporate understanding of what they hope they will accomplish.

One woman I know, Joann, had attended her women's group for four sessions, but she had missed the very first meeting. One weekend, Joann's cousin was in town and Joann invited her to the group meeting. When Joann arrived at the meeting space, she was surprised to find that the person who was supposed to share that night, Laurie, was cool and distant. Laurie left early, and the leader announced they would do something different that evening.

What went wrong? Either the group had not set the boundaries, such as clearly stating that new members or guests were not allowed unless the group agreed in advance, or they set that parameter in place on the first night and did not tell Joann about it. As a result, Joann and Laurie had to work through a misunderstanding that could have easily been avoided.

Just as critical to the health and longevity of a group is establishing how people will be treated. That may involve overt conversations about the ways in which the group will have conversation, prayer, and sharing. But it will also involve thinking about the leadership style of the group. Will people be able to take the conversation in a direction different from the one planned by the leader? Will there be a place for doubts and questions?

In truth, this stage is less about the "rules of engagement" and more about creating a safe place. Each person coming to the group will arrive with questions such as, "Will these people be honest?" "Will someone protect me from potential harm in this place?" "Will my story and contribution be honored here?"

Borrowing from the old sitcom *Cheers*, we all want to be in a place where "everyone knows our name and they're always glad we came." This gets lived out when groups develop a set of norms that guide the relationships between members. One of the essential norms is confidentiality, the promise that the stories, ideas, and emotions shared in a space will stay in that place. Confidences are kept. Most of us know that gossip destroys community, but a simple mandate not to gossip is not clear enough to protect the group members. Confidentiality needs to be defined and practiced with clarity and purpose.[10]

Confidentiality is allowing each person to offer her story to those people sitting in the room. Unless the story-sharer says differently, it should be expected that it go no further than the people present, not even to members who miss a meeting, unless authorized by the speaker. No content of another's sharing should extend to other family members, friends, or acquaintances. This does not mean that when one returns from a small group one is supposed to be tight-lipped. As we tell our counseling trainees, you can share how you're doing, if it was a good meeting for you, how you felt impacted by others (not naming or identifying them). You can always tell the story of your time in the group, but in a way that allows the others to have their own stories as well. Once this kind of confidentiality is in place, trust can take root.

Clarity and direction on foundational group issues allows a group to thrive. Once they are established, a group can move into the middle chapter of its life. From that point forward, the group is growing together with a common understanding of their nature and purpose. There are rich moments of connection and intimacy that happen along the way along with the predictable conflicts, issues, and derailments that can lead to the end of a group.

Settling in: The pitfall stage

The middle stage of group life can be like the end of the honeymoon stage in a marriage. This is when group life gets real. As intimacy builds and group dynamics solidify, there will be wonderful moments of clarity and fellowship. There will also be painful times of disappointment and exclusion.

In the ideal world, a small group would impact all of its members equally. But in reality, there are often those who find themselves on the fringe of the group. Some quieter members may feel shut down by more vocal members and therefore remain at the margins, feeling little ownership of the vision or the community. Others may be vocal about their discomfort with the group or their dissatisfaction with the ways in which the vision has been played out. Still others may actually be excluded by more dominant members of the group.

Each of these situations presents a challenge for the group— the leader in particular. In the case of those who feel shut down, it is important for leaders to understand where that quietness comes from. Knowing that public speaking tops most people's list of fears, outranking even death, it is not surprising that there are people who would rather sit quietly while others do the talking. If I choose to join in the dialogue, I am taking a risk, because not everyone may like my opinion, and therefore me. However, if I stay hidden or guarded, I lose out on being seen and known and never really join the group. It is a bind.

Inviting all the voices present when decisions are being made is a good way for the leader to prompt more reluctant members to practice the risky business of speaking before their peers. I try to begin all my groups with a few leading questions that invite each person to speak to the group. This "warm-up" gives them experience responding to a few easy questions like where they're from or how long they've been a part of this church/group/community. This also begins the process of disclosure. Sometimes I ask them to share something interesting about themselves that no one else in the group would know. These simple questions help people begin taking down their masks and allowing others an initial peek inside.

Knowing how to gently handle more dominating personalities can actually be a bit more difficult. I find it is often easier to draw people out— most people want to be invited to open up to others—than it is to get someone to tone down their desire to offer ideas and insight. The group leader may decide to meet with the individual separately from the group context to discuss the person's presence and input. The leader can inquire about how the person feels about the group experience and their part of the group dynamics. It is wise to see if the person is open to feedback. If so, the leader can share how she sees this person impacting the group. If the person is receptive and repentant, he may want to come back to the group and talk about his way of relating to others. He might even invite the group to help him recognize times when he needs to allow others to speak.

If the private conversation isn't productive, then the larger group can get involved. But first, the leader needs to inform the person of this action, saying, "I hear you saying you don't think your sharing has shut down some of the others. I'd like to invite the group to offer one another feedback on how the group experience is going and this may come up. If it does, how can I support you in handling whatever comes your way?"

If the person is very resistant to the leader, chances are he will not be open to the group's input, either. The person may decide that he is not appreciated in the way in which he would like to be and therefore may remove himself from the group. If he remains, the leader needs to be strong enough to honor all members by not allowing any one member to dominate over others. In the next chapter, we will listen in on a group that is dealing with this very issue.

Another area of concern for group leaders is that of mutiny. This can often come at a transition point between the beginning and middle chapters of the group. It is crucial that the leader not over-personalize the attack. There are many times when the group may have legitimate concerns that need to be addressed. However, a leader needs discernment about whether or not it is a concern that needs to be addressed, or if it's really a separate issue in disguise.

For instance, some members may find the group's growing intimacy threatening, so they might decide to resist the leader in an effort to sabotage the group. It is important that the leader respond with kind strength. This situation can be a good time to ask open-ended questions of the group and allow the members to respond to one another. That allows the rest of the group to put words to what might be a group member's negative contribution or provide insight if the leader is at fault.

Those of us who facilitate group therapy know that some hostility toward the therapist is inevitable.[11] Anger can surface when, either consciously or unconsciously, a group member is not getting the magic cure she hoped for or the leader has not singled her out as the favorite.[12] But therapists know that it isn't the leader's role to make everyone's concerns go away, but rather to create an environment where group members begin to find answers for themselves.

Members will test out a group leader's strength, offering unspoken challenges such as, "Can you stand up to me? Can you handle me? What if I constantly disregard the group's norms or speak out of turn—will someone really deal with me?" Acting wisely, not defensively, will serve to earn the respect of the warring members as well as the others in the group.

For example, Sharon always had issues with authority figures in her life. Whether it was her parents, schoolteachers, bosses, or even God, she always felt suspicious of those with power. Given those feelings, she often argued and challenged those in charge in an effort to gain strength by reducing theirs. When Sharon lived out this life pattern in her small group, everyone felt silenced.

Ron was the leader of the group. He felt like they accepted him quite well, even though he was 20 years their senior. One night Sharon leaned forward in her seat and said, "I disagree with what you're saying, and in fact, we haven't appreciated how you have led this group. It feels like an ego trip for you."

Ron was stunned. The group was quiet and looked confused. Ron could have tried to defend his point and remind Sharon that the leadership of the group was decided by all the members. In fact, he often made a point of offering minimal input in the group discussions. Instead, Ron took a deep breath. He waited until he knew he could speak without sounding defensive and asked Sharon if she could put more words to the ways in which she has felt discouraged by his leadership. He wisely shifted her complaint onto her shoulders rather than making it about the group.

Sharon had expected a head-to-head battle, so Ron's concern and nondefensive stance caught her off guard. "Well…like last week you commented on Tim's lateness and made him talk about it. That was mean and unfair."

Ron nodded and looked at Tim. "Let's check in with Tim about this directly. Tim, did you feel wronged last week?"

Tim was more than ready to respond. "The first week I had asked the group to tell me if I am living out my 'need-to-be-late' pattern here because I have had a bad habit of doing so. Actually I was glad that Ron gave me a chance to talk about what happened that day, because I felt a lot of shame coming in late and not being sure I would be able to tell everyone why."

Sharon shifted in her seat, visibly uncomfortable. Ron asked, "Sharon, are there any other issues you want to address as a group? I want you to be comfortable and feel you can participate with my leadership."

Sharon shrugged and said, "Well, if Tim is fine with it, then I guess I'm okay. I know I have a tendency to fly off the handle at times and maybe this was one of those times."

Ron knew those words were difficult for Sharon to say. He was genuinely open when he replied, "I would be happy to discuss any concerns you might have in whatever setting is most comfortable. I am glad you spoke up and didn't let those feelings fester. It also gave Tim a chance to share how he felt in case others in the group had similar concerns. Thanks for speaking up, Sharon."

As difficult as these kinds of issues can be, they can provide real breakthroughs for a small group. Group members need to know that the group can deal with internal conflict, hurt feelings, even outright anger between members and still come together as the body of Christ. These difficult times can do as much to build trust as the most intimate conversations.

Time to say goodbye: The closing stage

Saying goodbye is difficult for everyone. It is made even more difficult by the fact that few of us have ever had the experience of ending something well. Think of what you've done when you know a friend is leaving or when a loved one is dying. Most people gradually begin calling less, visiting less, slowly breaking the existing bond. We find other people with whom to share our intimate stories and meaningful experiences. When this happens in a marriage where one partner is dying, it is called "anticipatory grief." That means the surviving spouse anticipates losing the other and starts withdrawing (even unconsciously) as a way to protect himself from the full impact of the loss. This is normal behavior but can go in unhealthy directions if the person does not stay open to the reality of grief and loss, or to the opportunity to still love the person they are losing.

Good termination means allowing the end to be hard, knowing it will provoke grief and sorrow. That means one has loved well. It is also a time for remembering. This is true whether it is two friends parting or a group ending; we have a chance to tell one another what we have meant to each other.

In a group setting, it is best if the leader prepares the group for the ending several weeks in advance and gives them an opportunity to commemorate that time well. For instance, the leader may invite people to bring something to the last meeting that symbolizes what they've learned about themselves and/or the other members of the group. (It's helpful if the leader gives them some parameters for doing so. Some examples of this include buying a gift for themselves that speaks to what the group has meant to them, writing a few lines down in a card for each person present, or offering them words that capture who they have seen the other member to be during their journey together.) It is best if people prepare for that time rather than offering off-the-cuff remarks for their last gathering. This preparation invites them to experience the sadness of ending and allows them to celebrate as well as to feel sorrow at the end.

Some of life's richest treasures come at the end. Think of the life scenes that bring tears to your eyes: hospital bed confessions of love, spouses waving goodbye when one goes off to war, families standing with arms around each other at a freshly-covered gravesite, lovers parting in an airport, friends hugging after graduation, not sure when they will see each other again. Endings break our hearts with sadness and beauty. They are opportunities to speak words to one another that can have lasting impact. We can choose to take the risk to end well for the fruit it can be in our lives and others, or we can let the pain of goodbye keep us safe, guarded, nonchalant, and avoidant.

The positive power of a good ending is that it can change how we do other endings in our lives. Therefore, the leader has an important opportunity to invite members into a new way of relating to the many endings in all of our lives.

How a group starts is telling and significant for its entire life. Norm-setting, vision-building, offering supportive feedback and a place for all to be known is part of a healthy group's beginning. These will go a long way in helping the group weather the bumps that group life will inevitably bring. As the group progresses from the beginning stages of dreaming together through the maturing stages of conflict and learning to work together, it is preparing its members for the time when they will say goodbye to the journey that has helped shape their lives and left them changed.

SECTION 2

SPIRITUAL DIRECTION: REVIVING AN ANCIENT ART

A TALE OF SPIRITUAL DIRECTION

Anna approached the imposing stone entranceway to the place that would become her home for the next three years. Across the front of the tree-lined drive stood a tall ivy-covered archway with the name of the evangelical seminary carved deep into the stone. She felt daunted by the majesty of this academic setting and all that would be required from her as a student. "I hope I can keep up," she muttered under her breath as she drove her car onto campus and found her way to the school office.

It had been several years since she'd been in college, yet Anna recalled that freshman anxiety about not knowing where she was going and what she should be doing and wishing she did not look so nervous when upperclassmen passed her. She noticed there were many more men than women. That would please her parents, who were hoping graduate school might be a place for her to find "Mr. Right." She was not sure what she was doing there, apart from a nagging sense that she had been called by God.

What is a call? She read a few books on the topic and asked several friends in a Bible study who were also considering seminary. One friend, whose father was a minister, shared, "It is something you can't help but follow." That was enough for Anna. After receiving her admittance letter, she left her sales job, packed her car, and drove alone toward her future. "I wonder if this wasn't all some big mistake," Anna wondered as she drove. Her hope was that God would make the path clear for her in the days ahead.

As she started diving into theology, church history, exegesis work, and leadership courses, Anna felt like she was drowning in a sea of new vocabulary and a complexity that she had not bargained for when deciding to leave everything for seminary studies. She confided in a roommate, an upper-class student named Julia.

"What do you do when you find yourself knee-deep in books, not sure why you are here, asking questions of God and faith you never knew to ask before? How do you keep going?"

Julia gave her a knowing smile and said, "There were many days I wasn't sure what I believed anymore and wondered if I should give it all up and go to law school. Actually, I have ordered law school applications several times but ended up throwing them all away."

"That makes me feel less crazy. What has kept you sane, or at least kept you here?"

"Actually, I asked the minister at the church I attend if he knew of anyone I could talk to from time to time about my questions of God. He suggested *a local monastery of Benedictine nuns who were available for just such help. A number of people he knew in ministry found it very helpful and enriching. I was not sure about it but thought it was worth a try. The woman I see there is Sister Katherine. Let me give you their number and you can see who's available."*

"Thanks, I would really appreciate that and will give it a try."

Anna felt a lot less confident as she entered the mahogany-lined hallways of the monastery. There was a hush and reverent silence about the place. "I wonder how a nun will handle a woman going through seminary?" she mused as the woman who answered the door led her to the library where she would meet Sister Katherine. Anna took a deep breath and followed her into the room.

As Anna took her seat, she was pleasantly surprised at the kind face of the woman looking back at her. Anna realized, "I think I'm going to like her, and this may be a place to dive into my questions."

That proved to be true for Anna. Not only did she continue with Sister Katherine in direction, but she also joined a discernment group that was offered through the monastery. She was surprised and pleased to find herself in a diverse group of women trying to discern religious vocations as well as career decisions.

As she wrestled with which degree program to take and where in the world God might be calling her after graduation, others came with questions about marriage, work, and God's existence. Each member had a desire to get closer to God. The group was contemplative in style, providing much space for silent prayer, devotional reading of Scripture, and opportunities for people to share and give feedback to one another. Whenever Anna left the group, she felt a deep sense of calm, peacefulness, and hope. These feelings were in contrast to a full life and schedule. She was grateful for the space the group created for her. The goodness of the group helped Anna discern how to limit her busy schedule and live more intentionally. She found more room in her life for service and knew her relationships with others were deepened as well.

Throughout her seminary career, as classes helped her learn to dissect the truth, she found the contemplative practices of prayer, meditation, journaling, and devotional exercises invited her back to the voice of God that led her to seminary in the first place.[13] After her first year of individual and group direction, Anna was convinced of the value of direction and was confident she would pursue it for the rest of her life. She told her friend Julia, "Whatever ministry I am involved in, I can't imagine staying spiritually refreshed and alive without a director who is inviting me back to my own story and God's invitation in it."

CHAPTER SIX

THE CHALLENGES OF
SPIRITUAL DIRECTION

The first part of this book has been a guide through some of the basics of small group leadership—understanding the role of the small group, creating a healthy group environment, dealing with the phases of group dynamics. But for a small group to be a truly life-changing place for its participants, there needs to be an intentional focus on spiritual formation. While many small group facilitators shy away from taking on the role of "spiritual leader," I find helping leaders see themselves as spiritual directors frees them to use their gifts in ways they never expected. When a small group leader acts as a spiritual director, there is tremendous benefit for the entire group.

In recent years, there has been a renewed interest in the ancient art of spiritual direction, even in evangelical circles. There is a sense that this centuries-old practice can have a fresh relevance to the hungering hearts and minds of contemporary Christians.

Spiritual direction has been used in religious communities for generations: in the desert with the Ammas and Abbas of the 4th century, in medieval cloisters, in the homes of 17th century Puritans, and in modern-day offices where two people sit prayerfully seeking to live within God's plans. While the ancient sensibility of spiritual direction can make some evangelicals nervous, there is ample biblical support for the idea of one believer mentoring another. Take, for example, Eli and Samuel. In 1 Samuel 3:1-10, we find Eli guiding his young initiate:

The boy Samuel ministered before the LORD under Eli. In those days the word of the LORD was rare; there were not many visions.

One night Eli, whose eyes were becoming so weak that he could barely see, was lying down in his usual place. The lamp of God had not yet gone out, and Samuel was lying down in the temple of the LORD, where the ark of God was. Then the LORD called Samuel.

Samuel answered, "Here I am." And he ran to Eli and said, "Here I am; you called me."

But Eli said, "I did not call; go back and lie down." So he went and lay down.

Again the LORD called, "Samuel!" And Samuel got up and went to Eli and said, "Here I am; you called me."

"My son," Eli said, "I did not call; go back and lie down." Now Samuel did not yet know the LORD: The word of the LORD had not yet been revealed to him.

The LORD called Samuel a third time, and Samuel got up and went to Eli and said, "Here I am; you called me."

Then Eli realized that the LORD was calling the boy. So Eli told Samuel, "Go and lie down, and if he calls you, say, 'Speak, LORD, for your servant is listening.'" So Samuel went and lay down in his place.

The LORD came and stood there, calling as at the other times, "Samuel! Samuel!"

Then Samuel said, "Speak, for your servant is listening."

In this passage, God is literally calling Samuel, but Samuel does not recognize God's voice. It is Eli who, after numerous interruptions to his sleep, realizes this call is different. But Eli doesn't pull rank on Samuel. He doesn't say, "Let me handle this. You can watch as I take care of any incoming divine business for this household." Instead, he simply instructs Samuel to await another call and give a reply. In doing so, Eli invites Samuel to open his heart and mind to the possibility that not only does God exist but that God also wants to bless and speak directly to him.

That is what spiritual direction is all about. It is pointing out God to someone who might not recognize God's voice. It is creating openness in others so they can come to a deeper awareness of God's presence and invitation to live in faith. It is shifting their ears to hear a melody that previously played only in the background of their lives.

There are many modern voices that have attempted to put words to the mystery of two souls journeying to God. Each has its own way of expressing the dimensions of direction. In Kenneth Leech's seminal work on spiritual direction, *Soul Friend,* he defines direction as being "concerned with the mystery of the renewal of human souls."[14] He drew on the oft-quoted words of Augustine, who wrote, "No one can walk without a guide."[15] He likened the work of the director to one of discerning the motives of the person and being a shepherd offering healing and peace (in the tradition of Ezekiel 34). Leech defines the role as one of a confessor whose "purpose is forgiveness, not advice."[16] One of his emphases for direction is offering a cure to troubled places of the heart with discernment that allows directees to move toward God.

Eugene Peterson writes of direction as "curing souls." He says, "The cure of souls is the Scripture-directed, prayer-shaped care that is devoted to persons singly or in groups, in settings sacred and profane."[17] Peterson reminds us of a call to remember the past, times when doctrine and spirituality were not so fractured and disconnected. There is a heritage of Christian spiritual formation that includes the care of soul—a solid foundation built by the voices of old who point to the need for developing a sense of spirituality. This foundation is based on the idea that we must have companions on the journey to keep the embers of faith smoldering.

Direction as relationship

Naturally, the healthy interplay between director and directee comes only when there is a relationship of care and trust between the people involved. As noted earlier, we are created to be in community with others. Our Creator was not content to make human beings and then leave us to our own devices. Rather, we are called back to experience a loving bond with the One from whom we draw life and from whom we often run. We are known to ourselves, to others, and to God in the context of relationship with the Creator.

On a rudimentary level, spiritual direction involves two people growing in their understanding of what it means to love God and others. They are seeking the movement of God—both in the world and in their own lives—with watchful eyes and expectant hearts. They ask questions such as, "What is God up to in your life and in mine?" "Where is God's presence felt and known?" "What does God's voice sound like?" These questions, so often asked in the context of Christian friendship, have existed throughout the life of the church. At different times and in different places, relationships like this have taken on various names, but for our purposes, we will use the idea of two people seeking God together as our definition of the director/ directee connection. Typically, one person may have more experience with the life of faith and the other comes with questions and hopes for a deeper understanding of God. Still, this is a relationship built on mutual seeking and growth.

That spiritual direction is not based on one "teacher" and one "student" is in keeping with Christ's own model of spiritual direction. Certainly Jesus had a deeper understanding of faith than anyone else, but rather than working to impart his vast knowledge to the masses, Jesus led them by asking questions and opening them up to new ways of thinking.

The disciples' accounts lead us to believe that Jesus' followers did not understand many of Jesus' words and actions. Jesus would say, "He who has ears, let him hear" (Matthew 11:15). I imagine that the disciples were often left scratching their heads and saying, "I hope someone can explain that speech to me later." Like us, the disciples were often confused and shaken by Jesus' radical ideas.

I have to believe Jesus intended to leave some mystery in his words. He wanted people to find truth, not simply attach themselves to someone else's version of truth. He didn't take out a detailed map and give his listeners a clear-cut path to faith. He spoke in stories and invited people to follow him if they wanted to find more. Jesus provides an inspiring example of what it means to invite participation rather than demand conformity.

An effective spiritual director is one who is comfortable with the doubts and questions of the directee. No spiritual director will have all the answers to the profound questions of life and faith. But those who truly wish to draw others to faith can follow Jesus' example of offering an invitation to a deeper life of faith, one in which there is room for the mystery and wonder of God.

Direction across denominations

Catholic and Anglican traditions have long embraced the notion of spiritual direction. In recent years, other denominations have incorporated the practice into their communities as well. However, spiritual direction has not fully bridged all denominational divides. For some evangelical Christians, the term itself is misunderstood and mistrusted. Yet the traditional paradigm of caring for souls is beginning to make its way into more conservative churches. Gradually, many evangelicals are seeing the value of having others walk beside us on the journey of faith.

Even those leaders who operate in more liberal churches or outside of a formal church setting need to understand the evangelical reticence to spiritual direction. Increasingly, small groups include people who grew up in evangelical churches only to become disillusioned with their "family faith." The roots of their evangelical ideas often run deeper than they realize, leaving them with unspoken—perhaps even unconscious—concerns about spiritual direction.

Real spiritual direction can challenge a person's presuppositions and his images of God; it poses a threat to his sense of theological security. While these fears are legitimate, they can restrict the possibility of discovering something new about God and ourselves if they are not addressed. As Tilden Edwards put it, "Where suspicion reigns, there can be a fundamentalist, sectarian reaction that restricts guidance to Scripture and/or tradition, refusing to accept anything as of the Spirit unless born of explicit past Christian piety."[18]

Ultimately, involvement in relationship with others and with God is a partaking of mystery. We can no more control the reactions of our spouse, children, and friends than we can change the tides. So it is with God. We are finite beings staring into the infinite Abyss. Any encounter with another, involving two subjects, can change us and alter our way of thinking. It is stepping into a position of vulnerability with awareness that we may leave the moment as changed creatures. When the other is God, there's no telling what will happen.

Transformative relationship is a primary dynamic in spiritual direction. The God we thought we knew well may turn out to be very different from what we expected. Our lesson plans, sermon outlines, and exegetical work may not have prepared us for an encounter with a burning bush. It is this kind of risk that is required of those who think they have found answers to their existential questions (in the church and in the Bible) and may not wish to return to the questions again.

Given their priority on Scripture over and above experience, conservatives will have a healthy dose of skepticism about engaging in new ways of knowing God. In that sense, even questions or doubts seem dangerous. Direction is not a prescribed plan or detailed discussion. The doors are open to the possibility of God's presence as well as the two parties' own discoveries. In that encounter mystery abounds.

To help group members develop a level of comfort with the ambiguities of faith, spiritual directors need to create safe spaces for discussing spiritual matters. Story telling, for example, allows the group to talk about faith as it really plays out rather than in idealistic, abstract terms. In time, the group becomes comfortable with the idea that they are in the midst of their own stories, stories that are far from over.

Let me give you an example of how a small group leader might handle the tension between group members who are in a place of seeking and those who want to hold more tightly to their beliefs. Jim is a member of a small group. He attended a Christian college and has been a deacon at his church. Lately, Jim has been feeling threatened by the presence of some seekers who have been coming to his small group. They're not sure they believe in a Christian God but are interested in spiritual issues. Jim is especially troubled by Mary. She is a 20-something who only wears black and says the most unusual things about Scripture Jim has ever heard. Jim wishes that David, the leader, would assert himself when Mary speaks and correct her misguided thinking.

One week, Jim finally lashes out at Mary when she questions one of his cardinal truths, Christ's divinity. Mary is silenced and someone else jumps in to change the subject. David looks around at the group, then invites Mary to speak about how she is feeling. Mary bites her lower lip nervously and says, "Fine."

Another woman present says, "If someone spoke the words to me that you received from Jim, I would feel pretty bad." Mary nods her head, clearly upset over the interaction.

Jim feels confused and threatened. He crosses his arms and sits back further in his chair. He muses, "I was defending the truth in righteous anger. I shouldn't feel bad."

David turns to Jim and asks him to comment on how he is doing but he does so in a creative way. David says, "Jim, I'm aware that you spoke words to Mary that were said because you felt upset and wanted to protect what is very valuable to you. Do you have any guesses about how Mary might feel hearing those words?"

Jim pauses. He had not expected David to be understanding. He tries to put some words to David's request. "I guess she could be feeling like I cut her off and jumped all over her for her ideas that I don't agree with."

David responds, "My hunch is that she wants the same the same thing from you that you want from her."

Jim looks sideways at David and said, "What is that?"

David replies, "To be respected for what you bring."

David did not necessarily affirm the content of Mary's statement but did describe how we receive one another in this context. Respecting what each person brings is a model of Christ-like care for those who are different. Interestingly enough, Robert Wuthnow says, "In most groups, tolerance of diversity does not lead to radical, unorthodox ideas being promulgated."[19] Rather, when we engage with those who have ideas that differ from our own, we often find ourselves refined in the process.

Many evangelicals also grow concerned over the idea of submitting to someone who may not be theologically "sound." Indeed, all spiritual directors need to find a balance between the willingness to take risks and necessary discernment. Mark Yaconelli says he frequently encounters people's fears of direction. He believes this is because our spiritual lives are "the most intimate parts of ourselves…(and the direction) term implies that someone might have control over something…[leading us to ask] 'Do I trust this person?'"[20]

Several writers have examined historical insights regarding the fear of another's authority. As James Davies points out, after the Council of Trent the Catholic Church modified the position of director into a "confessor/penitent" role which dominated for 300 years."[21] He argues, "It was the confessor-judge approach to spiritual direction from which many classical Protestants rebelled, not the concept of spiritual directing itself."[22]

This past reality has influenced modern fears. Davies points to the practices of Luther, Zwingli, Calvin, and the 17th-century Puritans to substantiate the Protestant use of spiritual direction. He remarks that in *Pilgrim's Progress*, Christians are depicted as individuals alone.[23] In avoiding being "under" another, there is a danger of having an isolationist view of the call of the Christian. The witness of Scripture is that faith for Israel and the church is communal and meant to be a shared experience, not a solo venture.

Questions also arise from evangelical tendencies that may need to be challenged. Power and authority issues are serious concerns impacting conservatives' openness to spiritual direction. These congregants tend to have deep reverence and esteem for their clergy; the pastor has great control and influence. This power establishes a great divide between clergy and laity. It is also detrimental to lay people's sense of their own spiritual formation and development, as they are wholly dependent on others for spiritual manna.

Ideally, it is the community itself that helps allay the fear of improper authority. When a small group leader acts as a spiritual director, she does so in the context of a group of people who have agreed to seek God together. Again, this is not a teacher/student model, but one in which each member of the group has a say in the lives of others. The directee, then, is not so much under the authority of the director as she is participating in a communal effort to seek God.

It is essential to have a precise understanding of the leader's role as spiritual director. A director is not a doctrinal instructor or minister imparting a tradition to a student. He or she is the fellow journeyer who encourages the seeker's self-discovery in light of who God is. Many spiritual directors dislike the term "director" and prefer words that connote coming alongside someone, such as being a "midwife."[24] The director is not leading as much as assisting in the birthing of deeper faith. The director is a friend or a wise mentor to the one in the process of rediscovering God. As Howard Rice puts it, "The guide is alongside and not above the directee."[25] Spiritual directors struggle with the directee, relying on God's Spirit to serve as the catalytic force for spiritual maturity.

Introducing the concept of spiritual direction to a conservative audience requires a background in more traditional definitions of the field. A bridge is needed to connect the field of direction to the life experiences of those less familiar with it as a practice. There are areas of commonality between evangelicals and the field of spiritual direction. Evangelicals stress the need for a personal relationship with Jesus. This awareness of God's presence in our lives is evidence of our need for a deepening spiritual life.

In light of the thirst for spiritual answers, evangelism will look different in the 21st century from the way it did in any preceding century. Spiritual direction can provide a safe house to those who are curious about spiritual matters but are afraid of entering a church. It can provide a context for questions to be asked and ideas to be explored outside the bounds of the institutional church. It can become a welcome to a life of faith that so many postmodern people are seeking.

I believe that spiritual direction can be a place of communion between different theological camps. As I have attended events for spiritual directors, I have been amazed at the diverse theological traditions and backgrounds represented. It has given me hope that there is a platform upon which the faithful of many different allegiances can come together with respect and curiosity about one another. The practice of spiritual direction has the potential to call each of us to our roots where the barriers of theological difference can be, even if briefly, transcended.

CHAPTER SEVEN

SPIRITUAL DIRECTION IN PRACTICE

Spiritual direction is not a systematic process. Given the complexity of the human soul, different methods and approaches are necessary to reflect the uniqueness of the person and situation.

Direction is about creating a space for attending to the voice of the Holy Spirit and discerning the call of Jesus Christ in the lives of those present by both the director and directee/s. Directors bring a heart for God, the Scriptures, various forms of prayer, and inspirational writings to the process. Wise directors are those who are grounded in theology as well as students of psychology. They should have enough counseling savvy to discern when their directees are struggling with emotional and psychological issues that are impeding their spiritual growth.

Good direction will help to reconnect people with their bodies and emotions. It can help a sinner to know God by grace with freedom and responsibility. As Kenneth Leech describes it, direction is healing, transforming, and reconciling as sinners are liberated from bondage as they move toward freedom.[26] This freedom allows us to more truly love others. Rather than seeing direction as a movement inward, it should be seen as the process of moving upward and outward toward God and others.

Spiritual directors are present to God and their directees. There is a sense that the director is able to listen with one ear to God and the other to the person sitting with her. This does not mean God will flash words on a mental screen or speak audibly to the director. It means she is attentive to the Spirit's nudging. She is aware of how she is being affected by the person's words and presence and listening attentively, trusting that God will make his desires known, even in a still, small prompting.

In terms of the logistics of time and space, one consideration is the meeting place itself. Directors often display numerous icons and art to encourage directees' faith imagery. There is a sense of creating a sanctuary with the space allotted. Usually a candle is lit whose symbolism (representing the presence of the Holy Spirit) may be discussed between the participants or may be left up to directees' interpretation. Usually in direction, the time begins or ends with prayer (although directors are praying ceaselessly during the session on behalf of those with whom they meet). Silent prayer often surrounds spoken prayer. Silence adds to the sense of preparing a place for an encounter with God. It is space for listening to the soul and engaging with deeper questions of existence, something people's hurried lives rarely allow them to do.

Leader as guide

For many small group leaders, the idea of moving from group facilitator to spiritual director feels like a tremendous leap. In truth, those who have the leadership gifts and spiritual maturity to lead a group are mere steps away from using those skills to serve as spiritual directors.

In his book *Reformed Spirituality,* Howard Rice notes that spiritual directors need to possess humility, a spirit of mutuality, a sense of anticipation, a holistic view of personhood, and a sense of persistence.[27] Richard Foster believes that to be an "ideal" spiritual director one needs to "Love God, love people, and love life with no need to control others, which can be destructive... [They] listen well, keep confidences, and are not rigid. Turning spiritual disciplines into law will kill them."[28] Foster describes a person of integrity, vision, and compassion.

Thomas Morris points out the necessity of a "level of awareness of God's loving presence that indicates if someone is gifted for this particular ministry.... [Directors are] recognized by others who confirm the gifts with which God has empowered the director."[29] In other words, the small group—

and the larger church body if applicable—takes part in affirming the giftedness of the future director.

This is more normative than regarding the role of director as a title or office to attain. Have others come and requested your input regarding their spiritual life? Does the lunch discussion move to areas of spirituality where others seek your counsel? Have others asked you to mentor, disciple, or guide them? Those are good signs you are recognized as having the gifts of discernment and direction.

While a spiritual director need not have formal theological training, it is important that he have a solid understanding of theology, Scripture, and his faith tradition. He needs a strong faith life that includes prayer and the capacity to listen and engage with the questions and concerns of others.[30] These qualities, in combination with character and wisdom from other disciplines, enable the small group leader to offer meaningful spiritual direction to others.

Finally, spiritual directors need spiritual direction of their own. That can come in the form of a relationship with another director, a minister, or other small group leaders with a similar vision. What matters is that the spiritual director continues on his own path of growth and faith formation.

As it is practiced today, direction has some common elements for many directors. It provides a place for people to remove the masks they wear, particularly toward God, and provides the opportunity to grow in dialogue and prayer. It is time "set apart" for the purpose of being in God's presence together. A director's heart can be a powerful gift to the lives of small group members.

CHAPTER EIGHT

SPIRITUAL DIRECTION VERSUS COUNSELING

Sarah has been acting as a spiritual director in her small group for the past year. Recently, someone in her group began to open up about past abuse and the emotional and spiritual issues this abuse was bringing up. After I spoke at a recent seminar, Sarah came to me deeply concerned about this person in her group. "I'm not sure what my role is with her," Sarah said. "I want to help her through the spiritual issues, but it all feels like more than I can handle effectively. Our group has started to feel like a therapy session, and I'm not sure that's appropriate."

Sarah's concern is surprisingly common among spiritual directors. When people trust someone with their spirituality, they often feel comfortable digging into emotional and psychological issues. Yet for the directors, these issues can feel outside their abilities. Many Christian groups find themselves in a pseudo-counseling role and are not sure of their place as the body of Christ in assisting a wounded member. What can result is an awkward silence or lots of advice-giving. Either one can violate the one who has shared. It is at this point that the group leader needs to provide guidance. In order to do so, she needs to have an understanding of the ways in which her role as a director differs from the role of therapist.

As a therapist, director, and professor, I have spent many years wrestling with the challenges of defining the differences and points of contact between these disciplines. While there are many similarities between therapy and spiritual direction, the two are quite distinct from one another. Understanding those distinctions is the key to finding the balance between therapy and direction.

In both settings, space is set aside for a person or group to reflect and struggle with questions of life and faith. There is a purposeful focus on the needs of one person over and above the other, and the content that's brought up can sound similar. Both are concerned with the well being of others. Both traditionally involve two people sitting together working toward the betterment of one or both persons' conditions. Both involve the client or directee bringing up questions of herself, others, and God. Clients come for clarity, understanding, and healing. At times both relationships involve seeking an awareness of forgiveness, and being seen, heard, known, and understood. The time and space is meant to help another sort through the unanswered, and at times unanswerable, questions of life. It is sacred space for reflection and movement toward something better. Where the two practices differ is in the outcome, the frequency, and the focus.

The therapist often works primarily on helping a client overcome particular problems. The director is focused on the directee's experience of faith and exploring the question of who God has been to this person, and where God might be leading her. Most small groups led by directors meet once or twice a month, while therapy typically takes place once a week. Directors look for the fingerprints of God in the life of the directee. Unlike most counselees, the directee is usually encouraged to do more work on his own as part of the growth process.

The small group, even one that is committed to intimate, honest relationships, is not a place for a person struggling with psychological disorders or deep emotional struggles to find healing. That group member needs to have input from a counselor, psychologist, or psychiatrist prior to, or at least concurrent with, their direction work. Counseling enables people to cope with life's challenges more effectively, work through interpersonal difficulties and past abuse, and function more successfully in their day-to-day affairs. Direction can be an excellent companion to therapy, but it should never be a substitute.

Some directors argue that until people have worked through these arenas, they are not ready to do the deeper work of engaging with their image and view of God. Their belief is that direction can be highly disruptive, and the directee needs to have his feet planted firmly enough to be able to weather the impending turbulence.

Kathleen Fischer is a theologian, psychotherapist, and director. She points out that it is normally directors (rather than therapists) who ask for clarification in defining distinctions between therapy and direction. She also notes that directors need to recognize those in the small group who might not be ready for spiritual direction. She believes that people with emotional disorders or unresolved personal or childhood concerns need to pursue therapy before taking on the work of spiritual direction.[31] Fischer sees the two disciplines as being on a continuum. If pure direction is on one side and pure counseling on the other, the needs of most people will fall somewhere in between.

In cases such as the one Sarah told me about, it is the job of the director to help the person develop a sense of what's appropriate and what isn't in the small group setting while still offering to help the person find the professional help she needs. When people are struggling, they are not always aware of the impact their words and actions can have on others.

As I talked with Sarah, I said, "It sounds like you are sensing that the content of this member's concern is requiring a lot from you and the group, which may be moving you away from your mission. Have you thought about speaking to this group member and asking her if she would consider seeing a counselor? She could remain in the group while she is in therapy provided you invite her to a discussion about her impact on the group. You may need to remind her of the group's purpose and help her think through what is appropriate to share in that context."

It sounds like "tough love" to invite someone to take a look at himself in the midst of his other issues, but people often find honest words and questions empowering. It says, "I have confidence you can handle my concerns and we can engage in such a way that you will feel loved in my questions and also challenged to see and consider the whole group." Notice how the director *invites* an inside look rather than demanding, rebuking, or belittling the member. The director provides space for the struggling person to discern if he wants to continue with the group, or wait until he is in a stronger place to participate more fully.

CHAPTER NINE

CROSS-CULTURAL CONCERNS AND DIRECTION

Apart from dealing with the kinds of problems best handled by professional therapists, one of the biggest challenges spiritual directors face is connecting across cultures. This is particularly true for small group leaders, who may be involved with people from several different political, cultural, and religious backgrounds. Dominic Maruca stresses the importance of recognizing these differences, saying, "Our capacity to speak a healing and transforming word to those who come to us will depend on our sensitivity as well as our honesty and courage. This is not a question of whether we will compromise our principles, but one of flexibility and discretion in applying them."[32]

Clearly, a small group leader who is sincere in creating a group that welcomes all who want to come will have little choice but to work with people who are different from one another. This multiculturalism can be a tremendous benefit to the group. Whenever we are faced with people with perspectives that are unlike our own, we have the chance to re-interpret our experiences and our stories. We can begin to see that God is not limited to our western ideals, ethnicity, and social standing. We can discover that the practices of faith are not set in stone. We can let ourselves be stretched into new places of understanding and appreciation for the host of ways God works in the lives of God's people.

Sociologist Robert Bellah described an enlightened perspective on the possibilities, saying, "American individualism is not to be rejected but transformed by reconnecting it to the public realm."[33] Rather than viewing the individual versus society, Bellah allows for a self transformed by and in relationship with the community. This perspective offers a response to the common critique that spiritual direction creates an ego-centrism devoid of caring for and encountering others. Attentive direction can transform not only the vision of the directee and director, but of the larger community as well.

Spiritual direction for women

Much of the new literature on cross-cultural ministry is focused on working through the often-enormous differences between people of varying ethnicities and religious backgrounds. Yet there is little information available for the layperson seeking to minister across gender lines. For women in particular, there are numerous hurdles to overcome before spiritual direction can take place.

Writers on women's concerns often focus on the lack of self-development and self-awareness in women. For many, there has not been time amidst the demands of life to stop, be still, and consider who they are in God. Often women feel they are living out a role, a set of expectations given to them from others—family, friends, the church, the culture—that gives them the "do's and don'ts" of acceptable female behavior. Although North American women seem to have endless choices and opportunities, many women still find there is something missing.

Searching for meaning in the church can often be a frustrating experience for women. It is not uncommon for conservative churches to exclude women from leadership. (This exclusion is not unique to conservative evangelical churches; many conservative mainline denominations and Catholicism refuse to ordain women.) Given this reality, women are often confused about their place in the body of Christ and the value of their voice when it comes to matters of faith and practice.

Finding our voice is a biblical notion: God's voice was the power to create the cosmos. Jesus spoke words of healing, freedom, and liberation. The gospel is the "good news," words spoken and tasted. As image bearers, our voices are symbolic of our freedom and responsibility to be creative, liberating beings.

There is a need for women to be given the power to speak, to test our voices and be heard. Spiritual direction provides this opportunity. In her book, *Holy Listening: The Art of Spiritual Direction,* Margaret Guenther offers a powerful commentary on the process and call of spiritual direction. With application for both genders, she brings feminine strength to the descriptions and analogies for the process of walking together toward God. Direction is listening with a sense of reverence, respect, and awe at God's work and the individual's story. She defines this "holy listening" with four descriptive metaphors: "the spiritual director as host, teacher, midwife, and woman."[34] These commonplace metaphors take on rich spiritual significance as she explains the empowering gifts a director brings to another's soul. For example, the idea of assisting in the "birth" of someone's soul is a vivid image for what it means to come alongside another in labor and to celebrate the joy of new life. There is anticipation that something wonderfully profound will make an appearance as both participants remain faithful to the process.

These metaphors for spiritual direction certainly aren't meant to exclude men from spiritual direction. Rather, they create space for women to bring their unique gifts to the process of spiritual direction. As spiritual directors, women can provide a model of spiritual leadership that is not tied to ordination or other formal nods of approval from the denomination. It is a way for women to live out the example of Priscilla (see Acts 18), who had a reputation as a spiritual leader, one who was so influential that a new convert to Christianity, the Apostle Paul, sought her guidance and direction. Becoming a spiritual director is a natural next step for a woman who often finds herself called on to help other women deal with life issues or who is naturally drawn to small group leadership. These women are the heart of so many churches—they are the mentors and wise friends others instinctively turn to for counsel. Spiritual direction provides these women a place in the body in which their gifts and voices can give life to the whole community.

For women in small groups, seeing another woman in the role of spiritual director can provide a model of someone who has found the freedom to use her voice on behalf of others and even God. The impact of that model cannot be underestimated. When women have been wounded by past church experiences, even if that wounding is a subconscious sense of unworthiness or inferiority, being in the presence of a woman for whom faith is empowering can be a tremendously healing experience.

At the same time, it is just as significant for female directees to have the input of male directors who are willing to acknowledge their movements toward speech, who can hear their words—spoken and unspoken—and can affirm their growth toward God and others. These men may represent the first male in these women's stories who is willing to participate in her spiritual development and efforts at self-expression. They have the power to undo many confining presuppositions of the past.

Group leaders need to be sensitive to women's stories and actively invite them to speak up. It is wise to note when a conversation has been taking place amongst the men (or women) only. At those times a question to the silent ones can communicate the hope for their participation. "I notice the women haven't spoken into this dialogue for awhile. How about if we check in with a few of them to hear where they are with what is being discussed? They may have some new insights to bring to us."

Leaders need to be willing to examine their own way of acknowledging people's contributions—how do they respond when men speak? Women? If this self-reflection reveals areas of presupposition or prejudice, the leader may want to dialogue with a minister or counselor about these views on interacting with women so that he can do some good personal work outside the group. That will enable the leader to bring into the group the best of what he can offer to all of its members.

Direction for the oppressed

Brian McLaren's book *A New Kind of Christian* provides a brilliant example of informal spiritual direction. One of his protagonists, Dr. Oliver, is a high school teacher. He is "directing" a troubled pastor and offers him these words to consider:

> If we've sincerely and honestly wrestled with Scripture…and if we're really listening to one another—especially the minority voices, the ones we might try to marginalize and ignore—we have to believe that we'll be better off, more in tune with God's plan for us, less beguiled by our own culture and its subtle ways of tricking us into reinterpreting the faith…That's why the black church and the Hispanic church, the South American, Asian, and African churches, and also the medieval and ancient churches all have voices that the dominant modern European culture churches really need to listen to.[35]

If we wish to see the ways in which God is leading us, we need to be willing to take a broader look than the one provided by our narrow cultural understanding. Without the harmony of diverse voices and perspectives, we miss out on the fullness of God. Those who feel marginalized, who are out of the good graces of the dominant culture, have a story to tell that may offend, but may also invite others to change. The idea that difference enhances rather than threatens relationship allows us to be with one another in honoring ways.

Many have been oppressed in some way because of their gender, ethnicity, socio-economic status, or political stance. They lose not only a sense of their own voices and the feeling they have been heard by others, but they also lose a sense of vision for themselves and their story. Spiritual direction is about restoring a sense of vision and voice to those who have lost their way. Spiritual direction is a place in which many have rediscovered their sense of hope for purposeful engagement with life. Their experience of past suffering becomes formative rather than narrowing to their growing faith. Dealing with the questions suffering brings about can deepen these existential questions and stir a desire for justice.

Dealing with people whose life histories differ from our own, no matter if we are part of the dominant or oppressed culture, requires faith and maturity. It's not easy to relate to people around whom you have learned to be cautious. The reality is that relating to any other individual, even our spouses, parents, or children, is entering a cross-cultural experience. They may have grown up in a different part of the country or in a different time with different values and cultural norms, and likely don't share our views on all issues in life. Yet in spite of these differences, we try to be respectful of those close to us. That same respect is required in the small group. Every member has his or her own cultural context. Those who have learned that their context is not as valued as others will naturally tend toward more suspicion. They have good reason to wonder, as they have often dealt with being misunderstood and prejudged. Offering them care, compassion, and a genuine respect for what they bring to the table can go a long way in healing the hurts of the past.

Practically speaking, a group leader can listen carefully for the spaces in which the minority voices speak. It will be very important that the leader invites all participants to speak when they wish to join in. A simple statement like, "Let's hear from someone who hasn't spoken up yet," opens the door to those who might not have felt invited to speak. It is also helpful to say, "You might not all agree with what has been shared. Does anyone have anything else you wish to add which could expand our ideas on this topic?" If the members trust you to honor their contributions, inviting words from a different vantage point can bring tremendous richness and diversity to a group.

When you are dealing with a multi-cultural group, it is important to have sensitivity about time and process. For example, in some cultures showing up or ending on time is less important than developing relationships. Eye contact differs in various cultures; if someone doesn't meet your gaze, it doesn't necessarily mean she's disengaged. Some will feel uncomfortable offering a different opinion because they value group or family identity over that of the individual. A group leader needs to be sensitive to these kinds of differences and work to make the group a place that feels safe to all involved.

A group leader should also examine her heart to see how she feels about diversity. This might also be a wise topic to pursue in her own spiritual direction. It's worth talking about the ways in which the leader's inner story and ideas enhance or shut down the inclusion of others.

A good director invites people to rediscover God's vision for their lives. Vision restoration involves helping people reconnect with lost dreams and remember their sense of call. It helps them recollect the stories of God's gracious intrusions in their lives. A spiritual director has the opportunity to be a force, not only for change in the life of an individual, but in the life of a culture and a system. Powerful structures can be overturned by individual resolve to push against what had been previously accepted without question. Empowered people can reclaim a voice for themselves and for those who remain silenced and afraid. They can work against systems that deprive people of the opportunity for growth, life, health, and freedom.

Spiritual direction must be a combination of contemplation and action. Direction is ultimately about equipping people to fulfill their calling in being people of God's kingdom working for God's light and love to be made known to the world. How we live on behalf of others will bear the greatest evidence of God's love. Vincent van Gogh put it this way: "The more I think it over, the more I feel that there is nothing more truly artistic than to love people...Christ is more of an artist than the artists. He works in the living spirit and the living flesh, he makes men instead of statues."[36]

The work of our hands should be done with artistry in ways that enhance people's experience of the good news. Are we about assisting in building up people? Developing their sense of dignity and worth? Will they leave an interaction with us believing they are precious in God's sight? To those who watch us, the power of our message is only as great as the evidence of its fruit in our lives. By considering God's invitation to our participation in kingdom building, direction provides a path for our action to be lived out. The internal work equips and enables directees to live more intentional and informed outer lives. As a result, many have gone on to offer reconciliation, peace, and service to their neighbors near and far.

Direction's commission is to help people deepen their awareness of God's presence and activity in their lives. It moves into the places of ambiguity and mystery with the story of God's great love for us. That story includes not only the one unfolding in the room at the moment, but also the history, culture, mores, traumas, and triumphs of a person's past as well as dreams for the future. Direction is living out a call to pay attention. We are listening for God's movement in us and in the lives of those we engage. Direction helps people ground themselves in God and deepen their self-understanding as followers of Jesus individually, in the group setting, in the church, and in the world at large.

A TALE OF DIRECTION CONCLUDED

*It had been a long day on her chaplaincy shift at the large metropolitan hospital.
Ten years had passed since Anna graduated from seminary and drove out the tree-
lined drive, through the grand archway, and into her ministry. It had not been
an easy journey. There were many challenges along the way, some that made her
wonder all over again if the choice had been God's leading or a great mistake. But
in hindsight, she saw that through it all, God's presence was clear.*

*After school, Anna attended a course in Clinical Pastoral Education.
She came to realize that she loved working with people at critical moments
in life (and death). She felt capable of standing with families in their pain
and grief as well as offering solace and prayers to those who waited on news,
surgery, and test results. Anna felt delight in both God's nearness and empow-
erment as she offered Jesus' love to those who knew they were people in need.
There had been plenty of difficult, lonely hours and times of asking God
"Why?" She recalled sitting with young parents as they grieved their child's
untimely death. Yet even in those moments of tragedy and loss, mystery and
confusion, she had a sense that God used her to speak words of comfort and
offer a gift of presence that went beyond what she alone could give. At times
Anna had journeyed with a director and at other times found direction groups
that were lifelines for her. She continued to find direction a place of spiritual
renewal and nurture.*

*One evening as Anna sat at home sipping a warm cup of tea, she began
to look back over her life and ministry. How did she get to this place? It was then
that the kind face of Sister Katherine came to mind. She had not thought of her
for some time now, but was also aware that the gifts Katherine and that first
direction group had given her were part of the fertile soil out of which she offered
people nourishment each day. Katherine's wise words started flooding back into
Anna's memory:*

*"Remember God has given you much that you might offer it to this hun-
gry world."*

*"As his beloved adopted daughter, with a king for a father, you have a
high calling to pursue."*

"Learn to love in ways that empty you so that God can fill you anew."

*"Imitating Jesus requires bringing God's light to our places of darkness
and the Spirit's presence to make a home there."*

*Anna reflected on the confusion of those seminary days and her questions
of God and herself. Sister Katherine and the women gathering at the monastery*

had offered her voices of kindness that dispelled her fears and reminded her of God's deep, mysterious love that compelled gratitude and a desire for service.

Anna mused, "Katherine would be surprised to see me today. When I talked about my 'calling,' we never discussed chaplaincy, at least never explicitly. But we did discuss my childhood and my asthma attacks. I remember when I told her of my repeated hospitalizations and need for nebulizer treatments, Katherine said, 'I wonder what God has in mind for you with this unusual gift as part of your story.' I was perplexed by her comment at the time, as I had never considered asthma much of a gift. Now that statement seems clearer. Perhaps she had a sense that God was preparing me to deal with people who suffer. Certainly my life prepared me to not be a stranger to hospitals or the fears and questions of being ill. What a redemption of my own experience to be able to offer comfort as I remember the caring touch of my parents, ministers, and friends who came to encourage me."

Anna decided to write a letter of thanks to update her former director on where the journey had led; a path that neither had foreseen but that fit perfectly with the gift of God's presence that she rediscovered in those seminary years.

SECTION 3

DIRECTION AS A SMALL GROUP LEADERSHIP STYLE

CHAPTER TEN

THE BRIDGE TO POSTMODERNISM

Part of the flavor of our postmodern condition is a new attitude about how we treat others. The idea of the "other" is as old as Christianity itself, yet we have lost a real sense of what the term means. Often when we talk about "others" we mean other people who are basically like us. But in the postmodern era, we need to recognize that the "other" encompasses the alien, the foreigner, the outcast, the outsider, the exile, the reject, and the unpopular. It is everyone who differs from me in how they think, function, feel, believe, dress, dream, hurt, and question. While the "other" can be frightening, the postmodern age can open us up to God's possibilities at work in those who are different from us.

This area will be particularly challenging for small groups that tend to be diversity-free. In 1996, Robert Wuthnow observed that while "40 percent of North Americans are in small groups, two thirds of those groups are Bible study or adult prayer groups...which are self-chosen and are generally homogeneous. Harmony and comfort are more important than grappling with hard issues."[37] In a group made up of like-minded and like-looking people, fewer cultural or ethnic assumptions that are incompatible with the gospel will be disrupted. Such groups miss out on the fullness of life with God's people.

An example of a group reaching outside of themselves and inviting difference is found in the words of Carol Lakey Hess. Hess led a Bible study in which one of the women was active in a women's prison ministry. This group member began inviting the others in the group to participate in the ministry.

When they started stepping into this service work, the group changed. Hess says a remarkable thing happened. "In opening up to these 'strangers' in prison the group moved toward embracing its own marginalized members and its own hidden brokenness."[38] Their experiences beyond the group enlarged their hearts and brought up new questions of God and of one another. People cared for those who felt like outcasts but received care from them as well. Ministry began multiplying. Being in the world changes us and at times redefines the face of ministry.

As I mentioned earlier, the small group setting is not only a wonderful place for Christians to deepen their faith, but in many ways it is the ideal place for us to open up the church to those who might be hesitant to come in. Doing so, however, creates some challenges that small group leaders need to be prepared to handle.

Perhaps the biggest concern in creating environments that welcome the other is that they will not only be influenced by us, but that they will bring in dangerous influences of their own. Christians throughout history have been on a pendulum swing between being too accommodating toward culture and being too separate, seeking refuge in cloisters, the desert, or the halls of church. We work to find the balance inherent in the call to be in the world, not of the world.

In my senior year of college, I stayed in the holy huddle of my Christian friendships. I was afraid I couldn't relate to others or them to me. I feared my non-Christian friends would challenge my faith and rob me of it. Yet we are called to live differently, to have lives that witness and tell the story of the gospel. So how do we bridge the gap between a place of faithful witness and a world that may or may not care about our ideas?

The art of spiritual direction can help create a bridge between our faith and the world in which we live. Whatever sharing the good news looks like in the new millennium, it will have dialogue at its core. As Christians, we find out who we are in dialogue with God. So it is in our human relationships. Genuine dialogue means being willing to listen and to hear others' stories, hopes, dreams, and fears without imposing our perspective, advice, stories, and responses on them. To paraphrase Henry Wadsworth Longfellow, if we knew our enemy's secrets and stories, their pain and suffering would defuse our anger toward them. Bridge builders are those who can listen without fear (believing

God is stronger than others' opinions) and not lose their moorings. The bridge metaphor means we can walk across without abandoning the starting point.

Direction is a mutual process which can deepen both parties' experience of God. The bridge connects us and may invite us both to change as a result. Direction respects the fact that the people we sit with in a circle or sit across from over coffee are "other"— they are different from us. There is a gap that needs to be bridged to cross over into the experience and worldview of another and to invite others to share in ours. Because they view the world differently, others can help us see the world and ourselves differently. Others can provide us with a mirror that could reflect our own hearts. We must be willing to see into another and allow her mirror to impact our way of life and faith. In the face of difference, we have an opportunity to enter mystery that reminds us of our need to trust a God who is bigger than our boxes for God. We are reminded of a world larger than our own.

The place of knowledge

To be on a bridge, we must have a starting point. It is, then, essential that spiritual directors know what they believe. While it isn't necessary to be a theologian to be a spiritual director, it is helpful to create a place for studying and learning about theology. There is a helpful image that likens study to a "cathedral of the mind."[39] Imagine a Gothic cathedral. It has great height, mass, strength, and beauty in its architecture. Yet it also has large—and delicate—stained glass windows that could easily be crushed by the weight of the walls surrounding them. But the architects who built these great churches added the flying buttress, an engineering marvel that holds the whole structure together.

Learning what grounds our faith and how our thinking has been shaped allows us to approach others with less fear—it buttresses our faith. The study of theology offers us the knowledge that it is God who is grounding us. It took me years to figure out that God is my anchor. It is not my grip on God that matters, but God's grip on me. God is bigger than any adversaries who want to damage my faith. God is bigger than my doubts and questions.

Ironically, these challenges to our faith can often strengthen our understanding of God. There is something clarifying about being misunderstood and even accused by others. It invites growth and honest self-examination.

It makes us check ourselves for arrogance and self-righteousness, for narrow thinking or unbending hearts.

The study of theology isn't limited to book learning, and certainly not available only to those who pursue formal theological training. Theological study can come from anywhere—a book, a relationship, even a crisis. Eugene Peterson writes, "Evangelicals have so stressed the missionary and evangelistic emphasis that they have lost the art of 'being there' with people."[40] The Bible tells us that all people are made in the image of God, and therefore all reflect something of that image. Everyone has the potential to teach us about God. Listening to others doesn't mean we become them or abandon our own place. But it does imply an openness to be transformed by something through which God might be inviting us to a new place altogether.

My personal hermeneutic includes the idea that God gives truth, and I need to be willing to explore it in other's ideas as well as my own. That means directors need to be prepared for faith questions they may never have thought of. It means that my role as a spiritual director is not stagnant—I must be prepared to move toward God through the ideas of others.

Speaking the truth in love

Today, the challenge for leaders will be to know what they believe so they can speak the truth in love. But directors also need to see truth in all of its paradox; it is theology and doctrine, but also beauty and mystery. Truth is so complex we can never hope to master it. We must learn to seek after the knowledge God has offered us. We can know some of God's character and wisdom, but we must also content ourselves with our finite place in the universe and God's kingdom.

Speaking truth in love helps us acknowledge the challenge of being earthbound people. This kind of relating is very hard for us. However, the combination is significant and necessary to follow Christ's lead. This simple phrase, "Speak the truth in love," deals with two common failings with which most Christians struggle. The first is our idolatry of "rightness." When we raise answers above people and only operate out of a position of "I am right so you must be wrong," we err on the side of the Pharisees. Rigid fundamentalism of the left or right ends of the spectrum can destroy relationships. When the search for truth is reduced to an insistence on conformity to dogmatic principles devoid of love, it does not model Jesus' insight into and care for the hearts of others.

Yet when we refuse to speak truth and only operate out of a weak kind of love, we have the potential to become either anemic relativists ("I will hold to nothing so I don't offend anyone") or heretics. Church history has shown that there is something important in knowing what you believe in order to offer it to others. The traditions of the past guard us from inserting our own twist on truth in ways that could lead us to harm ourselves and others. Consider the Jonestown massacre or the Waco, Texas, tragedy where truth was pushed aside in the name of allegiance and "love."

The idea of being truthful with others can be frightening, particularly when we are the kind of people who don't do well with conflict. Fortunately, we are never alone in our efforts to seek truth in our relationships. During my college years I had a housemate who informed me she was a "good witch." We spent a year together and had many conversations along the way. One day she decided to challenge me and asked me to tell her about my beliefs. Words and ideas came to me in that conversation I honestly had never thought of before. My experience with this friend taught me that if I am willing to show up, the Holy Spirit will do the work. I just need to be a willing vessel. It was God's work in and through me. She did not have a change of heart during our time together; however, I know we left that conversation with respect for each other. I was grateful for her questions, and she appreciated that I did not damage her with my answers. I trust God for the rest.

A wise person once told me, "Until I felt heard in my pain, I wasn't able to hear others who tried to challenge me on my addictions." This statement is a testament to the power of truth combined with genuine love. Conviction can happen when people know they are cared for and loved. When the small group leader creates a space for both loving relationships and compassionate truth telling, the results can be life changing.

To be a bridge builder, which I argue is at the heart of spiritual direction, we need to offer others genuine respect. Other-centered love is at the heart of the gospel. Perfect love casts out fear, enough so that we can love others in revolutionary ways. We can live with differences because we know truth not just as a proposition but as a relationship with a Savior who died that we might be one with him and his Father. We can encounter more than one side of an issue and not be afraid we'll be washed away.

Leadership revisited

In light of these ideas about bridge building and truth telling, the role of spiritual director takes on a different sensibility from simply being a new kind of leadership. Spiritual direction needs to be understood as a non-authoritarian role where the director sees herself as a companion on the journey of the soul. To be honest, our language for describing this kind of relationship is too limited to offer any fresh understanding; even words like "leader" and "director" are terms laden with power differentials. A new term may one day emerge to validate the role of someone leading the group while also equipping the group to lead itself. For now, spiritual director seems a fitting description. It invites open dialogue, honest searching, and the questions of faith seekers. There is a sense of stewardship of time and relationships that allows the whole group—director included—to grow toward a deeper experience with God.

Direction transcends theological divisions. I have attended or taught at seven seminaries or Christian universities. In those different environments, some students and faculty had disdain for others who disagreed with them theologically. I had the opportunity to be part of the dominant culture as well as the oppressed one depending on the context. Because of my diverse background, I often was considered suspect by all parties involved. Even though the people in these settings all considered themselves Christians, there was an undercurrent of intolerance toward those who dared to hold to theological ideas that differed from the status quo.

I see spiritual direction as a common meeting ground for differing theological perspectives, the ultimate bridge builder in this postmodern era. I once attended a seminar for spiritual directors that included a Catholic priest, a Benedictine monk, several Presbyterian and Methodist ministers, and a number of therapists. We were not gathered to discuss theological distinctives: mass vs. communion, women in ministry, the role of the clergy. Rather we discussed how best to help someone know God as both immanent and transcendent, and then to live in that tension. For all of us, the crucial issue became what to do with suffering, both our own and others'. We thought through what it means to love God and live lives of faith. Despite our varying backgrounds, we came away with a common desire to minister to others. When seen as a process through which all are nurtured, spiritual direction has the potential to unify the body of Christ.

CHAPTER ELEVEN

SMALL GROUP ISSUES

All leaders work out of their own character and story. This means that the depth of what they offer is connected to where they have journeyed in their own life experiences, past stories, hopes, longings, grief, and relationships with God and others. A leader who acts as a spiritual director understands what it means to build bridges, engage culture, speak the truth in love, and relate to others whose stories are different. Those are the dynamic spiritual gifts needed for small group leadership today.

There are specific attributes spiritual directors need to practice in relationship to those in their care. Spiritual directors offer their presence to others. This means they are not agitated or waiting to jump in and have their turn to speak. They aren't preoccupied with what's going to happen next or who is bringing food next time. They are in the moment, listening attentively, focusing on others in ways that invite them to experience something of God's abiding care for them. This is seen in their awareness of God's presence and their own reliance on God's Spirit in their lives and work with people.

Good directors try to find a balance of theological grounding and a trust in God's sovereignty and mystery. They are able to trust the Holy Spirit with the person's soul and attend to the Spirit's guidance about when to speak, when to ask questions, and when to listen. Directors observe not only the words or content involved in what people say, but also the way in which they say it. They notice the non-verbal cues, the pauses, the self-edits that people do unconsciously. Directors see what might not be noticeable to the speaker. They work to be tuned in to the still, small voice of God. In order to flesh this out in terms of group life, we will examine how a director as leader handles two of the most common group struggles: sin and disclosure.

Dealing with sin

A small group that operates with spiritual direction as its leadership model will not be a group that tells people what clothes they should wear, who they should marry, or what they should do with their lives. Groups that try to corral their members into "obedience" to a certain set of ideas, norms, and sensibilities run the risk of spiritually abusing their members. That form of leadership violates the freedom God calls us to. Jesus told people, "Go and sin no more." He did not offer them five steps to avoid temptation or give them a set of rules and principles so they could live this out. They had to figure it out on their own.

Some groups also deny the presence of the Holy Spirit at work in the hearts of the other members. They decide it is their place to call each other on their sins, extracting the speck from their brother or sister's eye and ignoring the log in their own.[41] What these groups of "sin-spotters" do is spread gossip about others (in the name of Christian love) without ever working on the broken relationship at the heart of the conflict. "Let him who is without sin cast the first stone." Who is ready to label another a sinner and stone him/her? Who is sinless among us? Sin is real. It needs to be dealt with, but to point fingers at each other and declare, "Here is your sin," denies the reality that God has arrived in this person's heart before you.

And so spiritual directors need to deal with sin in creative ways. They help others take responsibility for seeing or spotting sin in their own lives and join them in celebrating their repentance. Let me give you an example of a spiritual director coming alongside the Spirit's work in someone's heart.

Janet, a 40-year-old minister, realized her addiction to busyness was ruling her life. She was so grateful for her relationship with Sonya, her spiritual director, because she knew she was free to examine how this addiction ruled her and interfered with her deeper calling to believe and trust in God. In the context of this relationship she was able to take the "busyness" glasses off and work through her issues with dialogue and guided prayer.

Janet:	I guess I didn't realize how hectic my life had become until I snapped at that deacon last week. I'd had enough. I preach about faith and knowing God is good, but I certainly don't live as if I believe those words. If I did, I imagine I wouldn't take on responsibility for the universe on a daily basis.
Sonya:	It sounds like you're clarifying your sense of call. How has that impacted you lately?
Janet:	I am tired of stepping in and filling the holes so people feel they are cared for by our church.
Sonya:	It sounds like you're moving away from one way of operating in ministry. What do you think God might be moving you toward?
Janet:	I feel like I'm learning that I need to honor the day I have. That may mean disappointing people, but I need to be true to what God has put on my plate for the day. It has always been important for me to please others, but I am realizing in the process I am not pleasing myself and not pleasing God. I may even interfere with God's work in someone's disappointment by not giving them room to turn to God or others for support.

Notice that Sonya didn't shy away from Janet's sense of conviction but did help her decide how to live out repentance in her ministry. Sonya's example can help all spiritual directors guide their directees to a place where the Holy Spirit can do its work and change hearts. The group, then, can be a place in which the journey toward wholeness is respected and supported. It is not so much a place of accountability—which suggests one party is watching the other—as a place where lives are lived and struggles shared.

In terms of group life, the director may need to step in in order to prevent harm. The director functions loosely as a traffic cop, not giving out tickets for a host of offense, but ensuring that members are not left without protection. When and if harm does occur, the director works to make sure the conflict gets processed and the group moves toward the reconciliation and redemption of all present.

Dealing with disclosure

This issue hearkens back to the discussion of the differences between direction and therapy in chapter 8. What do we do with the messy stuff of people's lives? Ideally, small groups are places where people strip off their masks and stand emotionally naked before others. They bare their souls, at times receiving blank stares and an uncomfortable silence in response. What does a leader do when difficult matters such as personal struggles, issues of trauma or temptation, past sins, or present addictions surface in the group? These problems are serious and have cost many groups their energy and momentum. Some groups commit themselves to avoiding this fallout by establishing norms to avoid getting into situations that could make others uncomfortable.

For example, the group should determine whether members have permission to suggest professional help to one another. This can be done in gentle ways: "I wonder if you would find it helpful to talk with a therapist about this situation?" But there may be times when the leader needs to step into a serious situation—domestic abuse, suicidal threats, extreme substance abuse. Will the group give its leader that prerogative? The group should also create boundaries so that one person's struggles won't overtake the group's broader vision. The group might decide to limit the number of times one person can share during the month or suggest that members who want to talk about their issues in greater depth meet with the spiritual director outside of the group's regular meeting time.

Spiritual directors also need to model responsiveness to others that helps the group honor what gets shared. Sometimes silence can be a meaningful gift. However, it is usually obvious if the silence is honoring someone's story or if it is there because no one knows what to say. Directors should be comfortable with silence and yet know when to respond to the sharer in a way that tells her she has been heard. Quick answers and efforts to talk someone out of how she is feeling will minimize the person's story and close down future disclosure. Certain phrases can invite people to process a moment of disclosure, such as, "That sounds like a painful/difficult/frightening place for you," or "I'm glad you felt safe enough to let us know how you feel about this. What would you like to see happen here as a result of what you have shared?"

If the spiritual director (or others) feel professional counseling is appropriate, a referral should be made after the group time so the member doesn't feel shame about having spoken. It would be wise for all group leaders to have the names and numbers of different resources for those who need that information (sliding scale counseling services, crisis hotlines, eating disorder clinics,

AA and other 12-step groups). Most ministers and area therapists can provide that referral information.

It is important that the group understand their role toward one another in light of disclosure. When dealing with emotional, psychological, or spiritual content, members need to know what is expected of them in terms of care outside of the group time. This is where the preventative steps mentioned above can be helpful. For people who are often in need and who see a small group as an opportunity to have people take care of them, a group with clearly established boundaries invites them to learn healthier boundaries themselves.

In the agreed-upon norms, it can be clearly stated that members can pursue relationships outside of the group time, but no one is obligated to connect beyond the group time other than to pray for one another. That relieves the group of having to carry one another on a daily basis and invites the person sharing to take responsibility for his own story. Being responsible may include getting more intensive care through therapy, particular support groups, or pursuing friendships with others.

For those who jump in to assume responsibility for others, the group can be a place to repent of taking on everyone's burdens. Caretakers are invited to resist stepping in and fixing the lives of others. This allows the group to see that what they have to offer is valuable and worthwhile. They don't need to prove their lovability by providing for others' needs all the time.

A group that learns to handle issues of sin, control, and disclosure in a healthy way is on the road to having dramatic impact in the lives of its members. In order to continue well a group must begin well. Setting clear guidelines, discussing the purpose of the group, and dealing with issues before they come up all offer the members a sense of security and clarity about their roles in the group. The director will be able to model a sense of care, empathy, patience, and concern. Joining others while inviting them deeper into their journeys with God is the challenge of group leadership.

SECTION 4

NEW MODELS FOR A NEW ERA

CHAPTER TWELVE

THE STORY-CENTERED GROUP

Rob Bell, a gifted minister from Mars Hill Church in Grand Rapids, Michigan, preached before the congregation at Willow Creek, a megachurch in the Chicago suburbs. In his sermon entitled, "We're Over Here" he posed this question for small groups, "Are we becoming the kinds of people that when we gather God shows up? When Yahweh shows up there aren't many words for it. The problem with that is that today people can explain it."[42] He is inviting the church to consider an incarnational understanding of themselves as Christ's body. In other words, we represent Jesus. We are told the Holy Spirit indwells us.

Therefore when we gather, we come together as image-bearers, redeemed sinners, able to experience God's love and presence through our fellowship. We are also cautioned to avoid explaining God, and instead to allow silence and mystery to be part of our time together. In this section, we will examine several ways of living out God's invitation to find fellowship and mystery in our relationships with one another. We will look at ideas for creating space in the small group for the sacred and the holy to intersect our lives.

At different points in church history, outsiders to the church knew that to enter the church was to find protection. The church was a sanctuary for bruised, broken, flawed people. And so it is today. Small groups can offer that same protection to their members and their stories. This is a place where all are free to tell their secrets without fear of punishment or judgment.[43] The group offers safety, acceptance, honesty, and relationship. These groups occupy a liminal space. That means they stand on the threshold between one order and a new, as-yet-undefined one. The space is set for God to appear in and through us.

The merging of small group ministry and spiritual direction creates a new model for community life. While Bible studies and topic-based small groups have their place, there is an increasing need for small groups to expand their reach and become places with no agenda but to draw people closer to God and each other.

Jesus was the master storyteller. The Bible tells us that God chose to tell the great cosmic story not through a list of doctrines and rules to follow but through scenes from the lives of God's people. The parables Jesus told were stories that were often subversive, provocative, even ambiguous. The stories of life and faith are the substance of our journey toward God. That means your story and mine are dear to the heart of our Creator. We love good novels and great movies because there is something at the heart of each of us that resonates with hearing, seeing, and experiencing story.

Several years ago, my family traveled in Ireland. While I was there, I met a real *seanchaidh*, which means "storyteller" in Gaelic.[44] He was an older gentleman with a cap and a cane who leaned back on an ancient stone wall to weave his tale. He pointed to the field behind us to tell us about the Battle of the Boyne. Not only did he tell us of the historical scene but of the families that lived there, of daughters and sons, of scenes from the past and legends that were part of the living ancient story. Interestingly, *seanchaidh* are not bound to truth telling in the journalistic sense. They tell a story for the sake of a good story with truth thrown in to move it along and give it some substance. That may offend our sense of honesty, but the idea that story in and of itself has value is worth retaining.

Think of what we know of Jesus because of the stories about his life: blind Bartimaeus, scorned Zacchaeus, inquisitive Nicodemus, the bent woman, the rich young ruler. Jesus allowed people's stories to intersect with his own and offered something that could entirely transform the arc of their narrative.

Part of our call as followers of Christ is to become good storytellers. We are also invited to become good story receivers. That means we offer others the kind of respect and presence that Jesus offered to those who entrusted their stories to him. A small group centered on story is concerned with what has been, what is, and what can be when a person is free to dream into the future.[45] There are many ways to access the stories and themes of our lives. One successful tactic is to structure the group so that each meeting centers on one person. That member is responsible for sharing three or four scenes from the past that have been defining moments. The group then will have the opportunity to offer feedback, to ask questions in order to open up what has been shared, and to invite the person to hear how the group experiences him in the telling of the story.

Consider these responses to a personal story:

• "You mentioned some painful scenes but you seemed very casual about it. Do you have any emotions around these events?"
• "As you spoke of God's absence you sounded guarded. Do you think there is more there you want to explore with us?"
• "What convictions did you form because of these scenes that still rule you today?"
• "How has the past freed you up or bound you? What impact do these stories have on your life in the present?"
• "What were the dreams that got lost along the way?"

In the first few meetings, the spiritual director will need to guide this time and model the type of questions and responses that are appropriate. The group can learn and jump in as they feel more confident about engaging with one another's stories.

The story-centered group in practice

It was Clara's week to share. Ever since the group's first meeting eight weeks earlier, she had considered how she would tell her story. There was so much to tell, but because it felt risky, she wondered if there would be words to speak when it was her turn. Everyone gathered in their usual seats, but Clara chose a different chair that had been added that evening. She glanced at her former space, a small wooden-framed chair in the corner, noting how it avoided the light and was somewhat removed from the rest of the group. She recognized it as a familiar choice for safety. The blue velvet chair she now sat in was closest to the kitchen, a high-traffic zone.

After the usual announcements and introductory pleasantries all eyes began to shift to Clara. She took a deep breath, tried to overcome the quivering of her voice and shaking in her knees, and began.

Clara chose her easiest story first. It was the one about her favorite place in her childhood home. The magnolia tree had heavy, blossomed limbs which hung low enough to shelter her from the world stood against the back fence in her yard. There was much conflict in her home; she grew up with an alcoholic dad and an angry, depressed mom. There was much she wished to escape. Whenever she sensed impending tension, she would pack several of her favorite storybooks in her duffle bag, throw in a piece of fruit, and head out to the tree. She could usually stay out for a few hours before anyone noticed she was gone. When the tree was in bloom, she loved the smell of the blossoms and being able to see out without anyone noticing her inside.

The second scene took place when she was in high school. She was trying out for the junior cheerleading squad and overheard several of the popular girls talking about her in the locker room. She remembered hearing them say, "I can't believe she is trying out. She'll never get in. I think it is embarrassing she would want to jump around in a short skirt. Have you seen her thighs?"

As Clara got to this point in the story, tears she had never wept for that scene flowed down her cheeks. She was surprised, fumbled for Kleenex from her purse, and tried to get hold of her emotions. "So I left the gym that day and never returned to practice or tried out for anything again. I would never let others hurt me like that again." With those last fighting words, the tears dried up, and she shifted noisily in her seat.

As if Clara sensed she was nearing the finish line, she launched into the third story quickly, wanting to be done as soon as possible so the focus could shift elsewhere. The third story was about the hope she had for a new long-distance dating relationship. She told the group, "I have always wanted to be married, but I often find myself pushing others away and avoiding close friendships with guys. I know this guy is trustworthy, but I can't seem to open up to him even though I want to and I feel like I'm trying. I feel pretty good about my life right now, but I can't figure out this dating thing. If only men came with rulebooks, or maybe, if I came with operating instructions, I would know to open up my heart to care for someone and let them care for me. Well, that's about all I have to say."

Clara sat back in the chair breathing a heavy sigh of relief. She hoped the group would discuss something different and move on, yet she also had to admit that she looked forward to having them interact with her about her story. Would they be kind, or would they be cruel? She realized she had taken a tremendous risk.

The group leader waited a few respectful moments, then turned to the group and said, "Do you have any comments or questions for Clara?"

After a short pause, one of the older women spoke up and said, "I am angry at those girls in the locker room. I can't believe how cruel they were to you. I'm sorry their words made you give up something you wanted." Clara felt understood and said, "Thanks."

One of the men chimed in, "I really liked the image of the magnolia tree and wanted to be there with you, but it sounded like you wanted to be alone. Do you think you would still rather be under the tree by yourself?"

Clara paused. "I hadn't really thought about that. I guess I did want to be alone then, but if I had a friend, or even my parents had wanted to come and be with me, then I would have been glad to have the company. Maybe now I want people to be under the tree with me, but I don't know how to invite them or include them."

Another man said, "Well, I feel invited tonight. Thanks for being so honest about your story and asking us to be in it with you."

"You do?" Clara replied. "Well, that is good to hear. I hadn't even thought I was inviting you but I guess I was."

The group leader asked the next question, saying, "You mentioned your dad's drinking and mom's anger and depression very casually. I don't know if you want to go into it here, but that sounds like pretty big stuff. Have you been able to talk through those stories with someone?"

"Actually, I have told a youth minister, and a few good friends and I have cried over some of the hurt of the past together," said Clara.

The leader replied, "I am glad there have been others you have invited into those tender parts of your story. It sounds like those times of working with them have been healing for you."

Then a woman in the group said, "Let me give you some advice about the men thing. Don't chase them. Make them come to you or else you'll have to do all the work for the rest of your life." Clara grimaced at those words.

The group leader paused before responding. "Clara, can you tell us how you are doing with those words?"

"Well, they sound just like my mother and her dating advice, which only messes me up more," Clara answered honestly. "I guess I felt pretty bad when I heard them. Sorry, Ann."

The leader then addressed Ann, saying, "Ann, I know you meant well by those words, but I do think that falls under the 'no advice-giving' rule we began with. My hunch is that you didn't intend to hurt Clara at all, but you can hear the impact of those words."

"Yikes!" responded Ann. "I am sorry, Clara. I didn't realize how offensive my words could sound. But it makes sense that they have not been helpful in the past."

The meeting came to a close with the group members praying for Clara. As she listened to their prayers, she realized God had been at work in her story, even in the painful places.

Clara's story is an example of a different kind of small group style in action. The spiritual director modeled care for Clara without taking care of her. Notice how the spiritual director was sure to check in on the issues that needed follow-up beyond the parameters of the group. Stories from the past, mom's depression, and dad's drinking were revisited to see whether or not Clara had received any support in those difficult parts of her story. In a therapeutic context, these issues would be unpacked further, but in this group context, it was appropriate to respect her words and invite her to do some of the deeper work with a trusted counselor or friend.

In this case, the spiritual director served as a traffic cop. When it was evident that harm had occurred, the director stepped in to help the two women work through what had just taken place. Had something not been said, it's possible Clara would have deemed Ann untrustworthy and perhaps distanced herself from Ann. Ann would have had no idea how her words impacted others and why people were not as open or warm with her. Both women were given a gift that evening and were able to move toward each other in a reconciled fashion.

Clara was honored by the group's presence in her story. They were not asked nor required to fix her or her struggles. They were not there to perform therapy or provide advice. They were there to be with her in her struggle and honor her life, entrusting her to God's hands.

A story-centered small group can offer us new perspectives on our lives, helping us become more aware of themes we hadn't noticed and areas of hope that may have been buried. We know from Scripture we are called to love one another, which implies community, and it is in the loving that others know we are God's beloved. The invitation to love in groups is not a sugar-coated, positive thinking kind of love. It is love that is willing to sit in places of grief and doubt, to wrestle alongside others as they struggle with God, and to celebrate moments of goodness, forgiveness, and joy with another. Love embodied in these ways transforms broken hearts and heals fragmented lives.

CHAPTER THIRTEEN

THE TEXT-CENTERED GROUP

Like the story-centered group, a text-centered group gathers and takes its identity from a specific way of seeking spiritual growth. Yet what makes the text-centered group more than a Bible study is that Scripture, while certainly looked to and respected, is not the only text used. Any text that calls a group to assemble and consider themselves and their relationship with God can be part of a text-centered group. These groups might use particular books or passages of the Bible, novels, or books on faith development that include study questions. They might use poetry readings, songs written and performed by others or by group members, short stories written by group members, even film reviews that spark a conversation. "Text" has a broad definition.

When a group comes together around one of these texts, the members understand their identity as being formed in engagement with the text. The text becomes a tool for community building. For example, a group may decide to discuss the work of a poet who writes specifically about gender issues. The group would likely be comprised of members of the same gender as the author (but it is intriguing to have mixed groups encounter gender-related material as well). They would read the poem and then discuss the connections between their experiences with life and faith and the ideas expressed in the poem. They might ask questions such as, "What are the implications of this poem for how I live? How does it affect the way I see my relationship with God and others? What does it mean to be a woman/man in light of what we are reading?"

I occasionally lead an all-women's group. In this group, the walls come down and we are honest about the struggles of being women. Stories are told and retold about how we live out our calling as women and how we invite other women to do likewise. As part of our time together we read poetry. One particular poem has assumed legendary status leading to an annual reading of this favorite. After we discuss our individual reactions to it, one of the women inevitably insists that we enter into the poem in a chorus of voices. By the end, we are dancing with our words in a hope-filled chant.[46]

Another group may discuss film. They might begin with each member talking about the impact of film in their own lives or talking about films which had a profound impact on them. It will then be against the backdrop of others' stories (filmmakers, screenwriters, actors, and directors) that the stories of the group emerge and are told. There will be many opportunities for groups to grow together as they consider movies that challenge and even confront them, while also inviting them to see themselves and others with more honesty.

A group that uses Scripture as their text has some unique challenges to consider. The first is that not everyone reads Scripture through the same theological lens (which is as true for clergy or biblical scholars as it is for laypeople), so reading becomes a complex task. That very fact often unnerves even the best group leaders and makes them wary of venturing into potentially troubling or difficult passages with their groups.

However, there is a practice of reading Scripture that can liberate our corporate study. This method comes from the ancient art of Jewish scholarship known as *midrash*. Jewish scholars would gather to disagree, dialogue, and discuss the meaning of a portion of Scripture. The process allowed for differences of opinion, for the scholars knew that the debate deepened understanding and allowed for more than one angle on the truth of the text. As many theologians and scholars argue, "The text is true. Our interpretations of the text are not."[47]

With that in mind, spiritual direction offers another insight into text-centered group experience. With direction there is the assumption that the Spirit is present and active and that prayerful hearts can discern God's leading. When a group journeys together with discernment as the context and Scripture as the content, they will find new ways of honoring the voices of others and listening more intently to the Spirit's leading.

A long-established practice of reading Scripture individually or with a group is called *lectio divina*, meaning "sacred reading." This devotional reading of the text often follows a certain pattern, although time lengths vary. The chosen text is read three to five times aloud with several moments for silent prayer in between each reading. The hearers have a chance to prayerfully consider God's Word to them that day from the text. They move from meditating on God's Word to a deeper level of prayerful contemplation.[48] At the end of this process, which can take about 30 minutes, the group members can choose to share their experiences of the text with one another. (For suggestions on different passages of Scripture, see Thelma Hall's book, *Too Deep for Words: Rediscovering Lectio Divina.)*

Small groups can also center on the writings of spiritual guides throughout history. Spiritual direction draws on the wisdom of ancient and contemporary spiritual writers and thinkers such as Augustine, Catherine of Siena, John of the Cross, Teresa of Avila, Julian of Norwich, Jonathan Edwards, and Thomas Merton. Most of these women and men led active lives of influence and involvement with others. They wrote from their own experience of having an authentic encounter with God which shaped their lives and callings. As Eugene Peterson put it, "The mystics were often the whole people of our past."[49] Dealing with their rich contributions, he encourages his readers to:

> Saturate our imaginations with people like Teresa of Avila and John of the Cross, Francis of Assisi, Gregory of Nyssa; these people who really did pursue lives of excellence in incredible humility and a complete indifference in terms of what people thought about them or whether they had any standing in life at all.[50]

That healthy detachment from others' definition and judgment is a pleasing corrective to our consumerist, competitive, and fragmented culture. The mystic writers have described their experiences in ways that invite others to grow closer to God and to likewise pursue God's calling.

The text-centered group in practice

Several years ago, I was part of a text-centered group that met around *The Red Tent,* a popular book on the fictionalized life of the biblical character Dinah.[51] The group started up very informally: Three of my friends were heading off to dinner to talk about the book when I ran into them, so they invited me to join them. At our meal, we discussed, reflected on, and wrestled with the meaning of the text. We considered its relevance to the Genesis account of Dinah's life and considered the implications of the story in our lives as women. It was a chance gathering, but we discovered that we liked to talk about ideas and common struggles together.

Despite the miles that now separate us, we still try to connect monthly or every other month. We are at different places in life but are amazed at how our stories continue to connect and how much closer we feel to God as we sit with one another. Over the years we have explored other texts together, and in every case the journey moves quickly from the text to our stories. We talk about the faith questions we're asking, the risks we believe God is calling us toward, and our hopes and fears in living as women. We have seen plays, attended church services for healing, and shared holidays. When one person is absent, the group feels incomplete. The group is greater than the sum of its parts. I am so grateful for that chance meeting that blessed my life greatly.

Texts can be a rich avenue toward multi-layered story experience. In the process of considering a text, we get better at engaging with the culture and with others as we look more deeply into their words and works and allow those ideas to shape ours. Biblical texts allow us to develop a deeper appreciation for the larger story of God's people, a story in which we are invited to live.

CHAPTER FOURTEEN

THE PRAYER-CENTERED GROUP

Group spiritual direction is most commonly lived out in the model of the prayer-centered gathering. These groups actively attend to the work and prompting of the Holy Spirit as it plays out within the group and within each member. By intentionally creating space and silence, these groups provide an open window through which the Spirit can enter. Unlike the story-centered or text-centered groups, where members minister to one another through words spoken and received, prayer-centered groups listen with the one who has shared to hear the words God might be speaking. Prayer groups might choose to gather simply for contemplative prayer or to pray for discernment for one another. There are different models for what this looks like in practice, but in every case, the act of sitting in silence together and praying alongside one another is central to the process.

One example of small group contemplative prayer is a model presented by the Shalem Institute, a think tank for spiritual formation. This model, developed by Gerald May, Tilden Edwards, and Rose Mary Dougherty, follows a certain pattern of prayer and silence. The group gathers in silence and then begins praying together. They may use a combination of body prayer (some form of stretching or breathing exercise to "increase awareness," "relax and generate alertness and attentiveness," and "release energy and focus on breathing"[52]); guided silence (with a thought or idea to meditate on or just being in silent prayer together); journal keeping; rest (allowing space for members to reflect on their time); or sharing with others as forms of prayer.[53]

For spiritual directors, the state of one's soul is intricately linked to the state of one's body. The body's movement into rest and focus frees the spirit to be more receptive and open as well. The sharing time is the place for group members to share their experience of sitting in silence. How has it been? What blocks did they encounter? The group can respond to the individual concerns but avoids giving advice. People quickly learn that this practice of praying together can be a wonderful template for their own personal prayer time. The goal of these groups is to heighten their awareness of all aspects of life, particularly of God's movement in and through them.

Prayer groups often gather to support someone in a moment of decision-making. Dougherty describes the benefits of direction groups, saying, "People learn to listen to God's Spirit at work in them for others in the group. As they take the sharing of others into the resting place of shared silence they seek to respond to what has been disclosed out of that prayerful place. Thus there is collective wisdom available for each person to lend vision to the directee. A group affords the possibility of many faces of truth being uncovered in any given situation."[54]

While God is not shy about speaking through people on behalf of others (Nathan to King David for example), discernment groups make space for God to go a step deeper. They invite the listening process to happen in community so that members can rely on more than one person's "word from God." The discernment process begins with open, receptive hearts gathering and paying attention to the nudges they are given on behalf of others. Participants offer their words with an open hand. They don't assume they are right about what another needs. Instead they come hoping to be empty vessels used by God in that moment.

Note that these gatherings are separate from the work of psychology and theology. The focus is on the spiritual walk, not necessarily on the members' adherence to creeds or doctrine or on emotional and psychological insights or interventions. Those factors obviously influence the ways we relate to God and others, but they are not the determining factor in the life and process of prayer-centered groups.

The prayer-centered group in practice

Dylan had considered going into missions. He had been shaped by many years of service in the business world, and he knew his work had given him the chance to be influential in many people's lives. However, he couldn't shake the nagging sense that he was missing something. Ever since he was a little boy, he had imagined being in a culture with people who were different from him and bringing them hope and light. Over the years, his vision began to take shape. He wanted to help people gain the skills to meet their basic needs. He wanted to learn about and from them before offering what he had to give.

Then an opportunity with a local missions agency opened up. Several of his friends from church were heading to Africa for a long-term missions project, and there was room for one more person to join their team. But Dylan was torn. On one hand, this opportunity felt like the answer to a long-held prayer. On the other hand, he felt very connected to his church community and his work. He wasn't sure he was ready to give all of that up. Which path was the one God was calling him to?

One of Dylan's friends, Gail, was studying spiritual direction at the seminary in town. When Dylan told Gail about his struggle to discern God's will in this situation, Gail suggested they gather a group to pray with and for him. "The Quakers called them 'clearness committees,'" Gail explained. Dylan knew clarity was exactly what he needed.

The following week, five friends gathered in Gail's living room to pray. Dylan was nervous about what God might do through this supportive group. He looked around the room and noted that these were men and women who had spoken into his life at different points. None of them had hesitated to speak strong, insightful words to him or retreated from the truth in the past. He appreciated those qualities in each of them and saw how beneficial they could be in discerning God's voice and speaking truth in love in this situation.

Gail explained that the group would spend a few minutes in silence, prayerfully asking God to be present and inviting space in their hearts to listen to God's movement in their time together for Dylan. They sat in a circle with a large candle flickering in the center as a reminder of the presence of the Holy Spirit.

After about 15 minutes of silence, the mood of the group had changed. They had all become far more still, grounded, and reflective. Gail invited the group to return to a prayerful place of listening to what Dylan needed from them. Dylan began telling the story of his questions about call. While he had written up a one-page summary of his dilemma, he found that the initial prayer time had brought a few more elements of his situation into clearer focus.

Dylan shared from his heart and was a little unnerved at the end when no one spoke up initially. He reminded himself that this was not like other groups in which he had participated. This group was not rushing in with their ideas, but listening for God's ideas. More space and silence ensued.

After a time, Dylan's friends began to ask questions, leaving space between each one for Dylan to ponder his responses and await the way the new information or question changed the direction of his thoughts. Dylan was surprised to discover that while the group was listening to God, they were listening within themselves and the group experience. He began to believe that his own sense of call was emerging from within him rather than God writing down his calling on a napkin and handing it to him.

As the group ended its time together, Dylan felt sure God was within him, guiding him toward his life's purpose. He didn't need to worry that he might miss God's call if he didn't listen or look hard enough to the world around him. Later that night, Dylan's prayers joined with the supportive words, questions, and insights from the discernment group to cast light on his decision. Finally, he had clarity.

One of the courses I taught in seminary was called, "Discovering your Ministry Potential." As part of the assigned work for the course, the students were invited to live out this "clearness committee" experience in small groups of three or four. They were invited to meet and pray for an hour per person. They started with prayer, then asked one person to share a current dilemma (usually vocational in nature). The group then prayed and interacted with that person for the rest of the hour. They were to avoid counseling one another, but instead simply let themselves be used by God in the discernment process.

For some, especially the counselors-in-training, this was a challenging experience. They described it as trying to learn to dance their partner's steps. They had to avoid some familiar places and try to let God lead them toward thinking on behalf of someone else. Others said this was the kind of experience they had always hoped to find in Christian community and that they were looking forward to creating this kind of group again.

Prayer-centered groups offer a sense of immediacy and aliveness to the members' experience of spiritual practices. As Isaac Pennington, a 17th-century Quaker, put it, "[Christians] are like a heap of fresh and living coals, warming one another as a great strength, freshness, and vigor of life flows into all."[55] The members are entering into this practice of prayer and discernment together and are thereby encouraged to deepen their own prayer life, which then can flow back into the community. They are given the experience of living in a listening mode, creating space for God rather than filling it with words.[56] Participating in God's work in the life of another encourages everyone involved to pay attention to God's work in their own lives. In the words of Tilden Edwards, "If people come ready to be vulnerable to God's life in them and the world, if they desire more than fear God's call to deepening liberation, intimacy, and compassion, then we can trust that grace will abound, despite and through our sometimes fumbling and groping ways as facilitator."[57]

Each of the three group options we have looked at—story, text, and prayer—provides opportunities for growth. In its own way, each is about reawakening the members' sense of passion, justice, and appreciation for what they have and can therefore offer others. In the process, lives are changed and redefined. Groups have the power to assist a new birth in the soul.

CONCLUSION

Spirituality is welcome in the postmodern age. Faith is seen as a journey, a process that takes place over time. It involves moments of disillusionment and discovery and allows room for feelings, ambiguity, and mystery. As postmodernism announces that whatever the future is, it will not be as it has been, the opportunities for people of faith are intriguing.

We need to be sensitive to the cultural paradigm shifts around us. In approaching others, there is a newfound need to be honest about our lives, to tell our personal stories rather than some grand narrative that may seem exclusive, and to speak of the limitations of our ability to know God. This new era has opened the door for Christians to own our doubt and to stand with others who are asking hard questions of faith and spirituality. Small groups based in spiritual direction provide the church with a rich tool for reaching into the postmodern culture and bringing out its gold.

As many writers have noted, spiritual direction is a gift, not something one learns through training alone. Certainly there are people who are particularly gifted at sitting with others and offering some form of spiritual direction. However, I believe that all people of faith are called to honor one another and God in relationships and to be known in that context. In one's own way, each of us can be a spiritual director.

In a world increasingly disinterested in formulaic answers to complex problems, we need to search out better resources for thoughtful engagement with the culture. Spiritual direction as a leadership style is not just for deepening the faith of existing Christians, but can also be a means of deepening our relationship to a world and culture that does not view us as relevant. If a spiritual hunger exists, the call to consider the voices of others from within and without our tradition in an effort to feed that hunger is vital.

Eugene Peterson's words show the value of deepening one's spiritual life and offering it to others:

> Spiritual direction shifts attention from what I can do or say that will help or "shape up" this person, to what the Holy Spirit is already doing. Basically, what we are trying to do is recover the intimate

attentiveness to soul, to each unique Spirit-created person that is everywhere implicit in our Scriptures. Spiritual direction counters the temptation to impose abstractions on a person, counters the coercive, manipulative, bullying tendencies that we so easily pick up when we are sure that we have something that other people need. This is a habit that is difficult to get into our muscles and bones—especially given the wordiness and eagerness of the evangelical world, but also because of North American culture as a whole… By beginning at that level it is easier to counter the suspicions. All we are trying to do is recover a basic element of Christian friendship/relationship/witness that is fast disappearing in our culture.[58]

A small group leader with the heart of a spiritual director offers a new way of engaging more deeply with the issues of existence and the relationship between the Creator and the created. Direction offers a voice to those who have felt powerless and mute. A director as leader can begin redemptive relationships with those who have felt exiled and abandoned by God and others. She can act as an ambassador of the church to others. A small group leader with the heart of a director can encourage fruitful spiritual exploration and call people to move through their fears into deepened relationships with God and each other.

ENDNOTES

Chapter 1

1 *Dogma*, Dir. Kevin Smith, Perf. Matt Damon, Ben Affleck, Linda Fiorentino, George Carlin, Lions Gate Films, 1999.

2 Dave Tomlinson, interview by Heather Webb "Continuing the Journey," *Mars Hill Review* 18 (2001): 67.

3 Mark Yaconelli quoted in Heather P. Webb, "Introducing Spiritual Direction to Theologically Conservative Students in a Post-evangelical Seminary," (DMIN diss., San Francisco Theological Seminary, 2000), 60.

4 Henri Nouwen, *Spiritual Direction* (Cincinnati Forward Movement Publications, 1981), 10.

Chapter 2

5 For more information about training offered at Mars Hill Graduate School, Bothell, Wash., see www.mhgs.edu.

Chapter 3

6 Elizabeth Bernstein, "Do-It-Yourself Religion," *The Wall Street Journal*, June 11, 2004, p. W1.

7 Bernstein, W1.

8 Dave Tomlinson, *The Post-Evangelical* (London: Triangle, 1995), 13.

9 Brian McLaren, *A New Kind of Christian*(San Francisco: Jossey-Bass, 2001), 109.

Chapter 5

10 Confidentiality by any health professionals, educators, and ministers includes any information and story except when there are cases of potential harm to self or others, or suspected child abuse. These need to be reported to the police in order to protect the person/s involved. In cases where this disclosure has taken place, it comes under the "Good Samaritan" clause. Don't you like that phrase? It means doing what the person believed was in the best interest of the other.

11 Irvin Yalom, *The Theory and Practice of Group Psychotherapy*, 3rd. ed. (New York: Basic Books, 1985), 304.

12 Yalom, 305.

Chapter 6

13 For more on contemplative practices see books by Thelma Hall, Marjorie Thompson, Don Postema, Lynne Baab, and Marva Dawn.

14 Leech, Kenneth. *Soul Friend* (San Francisco: Harper & Row, 1977), 39.

15 Leech, 41.

16 Leech, 172.

17 Eugene H. Peterson, *Contemplative Pastor: Returning to the art of Spiritual Direction* (Grand Rapids, Mich.: W. B. Eerdmans Publishing Company, 1993/89), 57.

18 Tilden Edwards, *Spiritual Friend* (New York: Paulist Press, 1980), 93.

19 Robert Wuthnow, *I Come Away Stronger: How Small Groups are Shaping American Religion* (Grand Rapids, Mich.: Wm. B. Eerdmans Publishing Co, 1994), 359.

20 Mark Yaconelli quoted in Heather P. Webb, "Introducing Spiritual Direction to Theologically Conservative Students in a Post-evangelical Seminary," (DMIN diss., San Francisco Theological Seminary, 2001), 79.

21 James Davies, "Patterns of Spiritual Direction," *Christian Education Journal* 13:3 (Spring 1993), 61.

22 Davies, 61.

23 Davies, 62.

24 Howard Rice, *Reformed Spirituality* (Louisville, KY: Westminster/ John Knox Press, 1991), 142.

25 Rice, 141.

Chapter 7

26 Leech, 29.

27 Rice, 140-145.

28 Richard Foster as quoted by Rodney Clapp, "How Many Hats Does Your Pastor Wear?" *Christianity Today* (Feb. 3, 1984), 26.

29 Morris: Internet.

30 Fara Sister Impastato, "An Introduction to Spiritual Direction for Christian Counselors: Its Meaning, History and Present Practice in a Roman Catholic Context." *Didaskalia* (Fall 1996), 33.

Chapter 8

31 Kathleen Fischer, interview with author, February 10, 2000.

Chapter 9

32 Susan Rakoczy, ed., *Common Journey, Different Paths: Spiritual Direction in Cross-cultural Perspective* (Maryknoll, NY: Orbis Books, 1992), 40.

33 Robert Bellah and William Sullivan, *Habits of the Heart* (Berkeley: University of California, 1985), 248.

34 Margaret Guenther as quoted by Clement Mehlman, "Engendering Spiritual Direction: In the Presence of Women," *Pneuma* 2:1 (Spring 1995). <http://www.worship.on.ca/> (October 1999).

35 McLaren, 79.

36 Don Postema, *Space for God: The Study and Practice of Prayer and Spirituality* (Grand Rapids, Mich.: Board of the Publications of the Christian Reformed Church, 1983), 68.

Chapter 10

37 Robert Wuthnow as quoted by Carol Lakey Hess, *Caretakers of our Common House* (Nashville, Tenn.: Abingdon Press, 1997), 207.

38 Hess, 209.

39 Etienne Gilson, quoted in Alister McGrath, *Christian Theology: An Introduction* (Oxford, UK: Blackwell Publishers Ltd., 1997), 50.

40 Eugene Peterson, conversation with author, September 2000.

Chapter 11

41 Paraphrase of Matthew 7:3.

Chapter 12

42 Rob Bell, sermon entitled, "We're Over Here" (Barrington, Illinois: Willow Creek Association, 2002), audiocassette tape.

43 See Frederick Buechner's *Telling Secrets* to learn more about how this is made manifest in the group context.

44 Faclair Gàidhlig – Beurla, Gaelic English Dictionary, http://www.cmth.ph.ic.ac.uk/people/a.mackinnon/Personal/Faclair/S.html.

45 For more on the idea of our stories involved in the past, present, and future see Dan Allender, *The Healing Path* (Colorado Springs, Colo.: Waterbrook Press, 1999) and *To Be Told: Embracing the Stories of Your Life* (Colorado Springs, Colo.: Waterbrook Press, 2005).

Chapter 13

46 Heather Webb, *Redeeming Eve* (Grand Rapids, Mich.: Baker Book House, 2001) 94.

47 John G. Stackhouse, ed., *Evangelical Futures: A Conversation on Theological Method* (Grand Rapids, Mich.: Baker Book House, 2000), 47.

48 Thelma Hall, *Too Deep for Words: Rediscovering Lectio Divina* (New York: Paulist Press, 1988), 28, 36-56.

49 Eugene H. Peterson, *Subversive Spirituality* (Grand Rapids, Mich.: W. B. Eerdmans Publishing Company, 1987), 254.

50 Eugene H. Peterson, *Subversive Spirituality*, 250.

51 Anita Diamant, *The Red Tent* (New York: Picador USA, 1998).

Chapter 14

52 Gerald May, *Pilgrimage Home: The Conduct of Contemplative Practices in Small Groups* (Mahwah, N.J.: Paulist Press, 1979), 47, 113, 132.

53 Tilden Edwards, *Living in the Presence* (San Francisco: Harper San Francisco, 1995), 133.

54 Rose Mary Dougherty, *Group Spiritual Direction* (Mahwah, N.J.: Paulist Press, 1995), 36.

55 Edwards, *Living in the Presence*, 126.

56 See Don Postema's book, *Space for God* (Grand Rapids, Mich.: Board of the Publication of the Christian Reformed Church, 1983), for more ideas on developing and renewing one's prayer life.

57 Edwards, *Living in the Presence*, 154.

58 Eugene Peterson, personal correspondence to author, 28 July 2000.

BIBLIOGRAPHY

Dan Allender. *The Healing Path.* Colorado Springs, Colo.: Waterbrook Press, 1999.

Allender, Dan. *To Be Told: Embracing the Stories of Your Life.* Colorado Springs, Colo.: Waterbrook Press, 2005.

William Barry & William Connolly. *The Practice of Spiritual Direction.* New York: Seabury Press, 1982.

Bellah, Robert and William Sullivan. *Habits of the Heart.* Berkeley: University of California, 1985.

Brend, Mark. "Spokesman for a Silent Majority: Interview with Dave Tomlinson." *Christianity Today* (September 1997): 19-46.

Buechner, Frederick. *Telling Secrets.* San Francisco: Harper SanFrancisco, 1992.

Chambers, Oswald. *My Utmost for his Highest.* Westwood, N.J.: Barbour & Co., 1963.

Clapp, Rodney. "How Many Hats Does Your Pastor Wear?" *Christianity Today* 28 (Feb. 3, 1984):24-27.

Davies, James. "Patterns of Spiritual Direction." *Christian Education Journal* 13:3, (Spring 1993): 49-66.

Diamant, Anita. *The Red Tent.* New York: Picador USA, 1998.

Dougherty, Rose Mary. *Group Spiritual Direction.* Mahwah, N.J.: Paulist Press, 1995.

Driver, Tom F. *The Magic of Ritual.* San Francisco: Harper, 1991.

Dogma, Dir. Kevin Smith, Perf. Matt Damon, Ben Affleck, Linda Fiorentino, George Carlin, Lions Gate Films, 1999.

Edwards, Tilden. *Living in the Presence: Spiritual Exercises to Open our Eyes to the Awareness of God*. San Francisco: Harper San Francisco, 1995.

Edwards, Tilden. *Spiritual Friend*. New York: Paulist Press, 1980.

Faclair Gàidhlig – Beurla, Gaelic English Dictionary, http://www.cmth.ph.ic. ac.uk/people/a.mackinnon/Personal/Faclair/S.html (April 2004).

Farnham, Suzanne G., Joseph P. Gill, R. Taylor McLean, and Susan M. Ward, *Listening Hearts: Discerning Call in Community*. Harrisburg, Penn.: Morehouse Publ., 1991.

Fischer, Kathleen. *Women at the Well: Feminist Perspectives on Spiritual Direction*. New York: Paulist Press, 1988.

Gratton, Carolyn. *Guidelines for Spiritual Direction*. Denville, N.J.: Dimension Books, 1980.

Guenther, Margaret. *Holy Listening: The Art of Spiritual Direction*. Cambridge, Mass.: Cowley Publishing, 1992.

Hall, Thelma. *Too Deep for Words: Rediscovering Lectio Divina*. New York: Paulist Press, 1988.

Impastato, Fara Sister. "An Introduction to Spiritual Direction for Christian Counselors: Its Meaning, History and Present Practice in a Roman Catholic Context." *Didaskalia*. Fall 1996: 26-40.

Jones, Alan. *Exploring Spiritual Direction: An Essay on Christian Friendship*. Minneapolis, Minn.: Seabury Press, 1982.

Keillor, Garrison. "A Prairie Home Companion." Radio Talk Show, NPR. August, 7, 1999.

Krakow, Amy. *The Total Tattoo Book*. New York: Warner Books, 1994.

Leech, Kenneth. "Is Spiritual Direction Losing Its Bearings?" *Pneuma* 2:2, Fall 1995. (October 1999).

Leech, Kenneth. *Soul Friend*. San Francisco: Harper & Row, 1977.

Liebert, Elizabeth. *Changing Life Patterns: Adult Development in Spiritual Direction*. New York: Paulist Press, 1992.

May, Gerald. *Pilgrimage Home: The Conduct of Contemplative Practices in Small Groups*. Mahwah, N.J.: Paulist Press, 1979.

MacLeod, Duncan. "Review of *Virtual Faith: The Irreverent Spiritual Quest of Generation X* by Tom Beaudoin," *Crumbs Journal*. Winter 1999.

McKee, Diana Robertson. "Spiritual Companion: A Study of Selected Historical and Contemporary Writers on Spiritual Direction with Implications for the Role of the Minister as Spiritual Guide." DMIN diss., San Francisco Theological Seminary, 1990.

McLaren, Brian. *A New Kind of Christian*. San Francisco: Jossey-Bass, 2001.

Mehlman, Clement. "Engendering Spiritual Direction: In the Presence of Women." *Pneuma* 2:1 (Spring 1995). http://www.worship.on.ca (October 1999).

McGrath, Alister. *Christian Theology: An Introduction*. Oxford, UK: Blackwell Publishers Ltd., 1997.

Morris, Thomas. "Gifted for the Journey: The Art of Spiritual Direction." *Pneuma* 4:1 (Spring 1997). http://www.worship.on.ca (October 1999).

Nouwen, Henri. *Spiritual Direction*. Cincinnati, Ohio: Forward Movement Publications, 1981.

Nouwen, Henri. *The Way of the Heart*. New York: Ballantine Books, 1981.

Peterson, Eugene H. *Contemplative Pastor: Returning to the Art of Spiritual Direction* (Grand Rapids, Mich.: W. B. Eerdmans Publishing Company, 1993/89), 57.

Postema, Don. *Space for God: The Study and Practice of Prayer and*

Spirituality. Grand Rapids, Mich.: Board of the Publications of the Christian Reformed Church, 1983.

Rakoczy, Susan ed. *Common Journey, Different Paths: Spiritual Direction in Cross-cultural Perspective.* Maryknoll, N.Y.: Orbis Books, 1992.

Rice, Howard. *Reformed Spirituality.* Louisville, Ky.: Westminster/John Knox Press, 1991.

Richardson, Robin. "Spiritual Direction and Religious Endeavor," *British Journal of Religious Education* 10 (Summer 1988): 128-134.

Schneiders, Sandra Marie. *Spiritual Direction: Reflections on a Contemporary Ministry.* Chicago: National Sisters Vocation Conference, 1976.

Stackhouse, John G. ed. *Evangelical Futures: A Conversation on Theological Method.* Grand Rapids, Mich.: Baker Book House, 2000.

Strickling, Bonnelle. Instructor for "Spiritual Direction, Spiritual Life and Therapy." March 1999. Advanced Spiritual Directors course. San Francisco Theological Seminary.

Tomlinson, Dave. *The Post-Evangelical.* London: Triangle, 1995.

Tracy, David. "Theology and the Many Faces of Postmodernity." *Theology Today* (April 1994): 104-114.

Webb, Heather P. "Introducing Spiritual Direction to Theologically Conservative Students in a Post-evangelical Seminary." DMIN diss., San Francisco Theological Seminary, 2000.

Webb, Heather. "Continuing the Journey," *Mars Hill Review* 18 (2001): 65-77.

Webb, Heather. "Pain as Ritual: Hearing Voices from the Alternative Culture," *Mars Hill Review* 16 (2000): 49-54.

Webb, Heather. *Redeeming Eve.* Grand Rapids, Mich.: Baker Book House, 2001.

Webb, Heather. "Spiritual Direction and Counselling," *The Christian Counsellor* (Fall 2001): 20-25.

Wuthnow, Robert. *I Come Away Stronger: How Small Groups are Shaping American Religion.* Grand Rapids, Mich.: Wm. B. Eerdmans Publishing Co, 1994.

Wuthnow, Robert. "Spiritual Practice," *Christian Century* (September 23-30, 1998): 854-855.

Yalom, Irvin. *The Theory and Practice of Group Psychotherapy, 3rd. ed.* New York: Basic Books, 1985.

ACKNOWLEDGMENTS

For many years, I have been passionate about the topic of spiritual direction. As a minister and therapist, I've found it to be the thread that brings these two parts of my experience together. Along the way, there have been many faces and names, people who have helped me wander in these ideas and see that the spiritual direction model is relevant for small group leaders in the emerging church.

I have had the privilege of introducing the topic of spiritual direction to some wise and thoughtful students at Mars Hill Graduate School, and they have taught me a great deal along the way. All the faces and names of the students who have journeyed with me have taught me much about group work.

I am indebted to Brian McLaren for bringing my proposal to the attention of emergentYS, and to Jay Howver, who has been a supporter of my ideas on spiritual direction for several years.

I also need to thank Eugene Peterson, who journeyed with me as my dissertation advisor. His insights and feedback have been invaluable, and his influence seasons this work from beginning to end.

To all those who have traveled with me as directees, your honesty and desire to live in God's story have been an inspiration for me.

To my wise spiritual directors, Kathleen Fischer and Carol Saysette—I have been honored to grow in God through your companionship and presence.

To the Red Tent women and my clergywomen's prayer group—you have often stood in the gap with wise words of discernment and inspired prayers. Thank you.

For putting up with deadlines, editing my work, and encouraging me to live these words, I am deeply grateful to my husband, Kirk. To Alyse—thank you for sacrificing some time with your mother for the sake of words written. You are both windows of God's graciousness and love.

The Search to Belong is a practical guide for pastors and church leaders—in fact, all leaders—who struggle with building community in a culture that values belonging over believing.

"A simple insight (your true 'belongings' are not your possessions, but the people to whom you belong and who belong to you) leads Joseph R. Myers to some of the most revolutionary and original thinking about small groups in the church today."

-Leonard Sweet, Drew Theological School, George Fox University, preachingplus.com

Visit **www.emergentys.com** or your local Christian bookstore.

REIMAGINING SPIRITUAL FORMATION ISN'T ABOUT QUICK-FIX METHODS OR BULLETED, HOW-TO LISTS. AND IT'S CERTAINLY NOT A DRY LECTURE ABOUT A HEADY THEOLOGICAL TOPIC.

Inside these pages you'll spend a full week with Solomon's Porch—a holistic, missional, Christian community in Minneapolis, Minnesota—and get a front row seat at the gatherings, meetings, and meals. Along the way, you'll also discover what spiritual formation looks like in a church community that's moves beyond education-based practices by including worship, physicality, dialogue, hospitality, belief, creativity, and service as means toward spiritual formation rather than mere appendices to it.

RETAIL $16.99
ISBN 0310256879

Visit **www.emergentys.com** or your local Christian bookstore.